Indirections

Indirections

for those who want
TO WRITE
by Sidney Cox

A NONPAREIL BOOK
David R. Godine - Publisher - Boston

THIS IS A NONPAREIL BOOK

First published in the U.S. in 1981 by
David R. Godine, Publisher, Inc.
Horticultural Hall
300 Massachusetts Avenue
Boston, Massachusetts 02115

Library of Congress Cataloging in Publication Data

Cox, Sidney, 1889–1952.
INDIRECTIONS: for those who want to write.

(Nonpareil books; 22)
Reprint of the 1962 ed. published by Knopf,
New York.
I. Authorship. I. Title. II. Series.
PN175.C6 1981   808'.042   80-39820
ISBN 0-87923-389-3   AACRI

Third printing, March 1986

This book has been printed on acid-free paper and sewn
in signatures. The paper will not yellow with age, the
binding will not deteriorate, and
the pages will not fall out.

Printed in the United States of America

FOR ALICE

PREFACE

The act of composition is performed by all of us. Every time we make up our minds we compose. We change the composition of ourselves and of the world. Where there is life at all there is a constant forming. And the fun and joy in living comes when we make incompatibles unite.

Indirections—which also might be called Out of Conflicts Composition—is therefore not exclusively "for those who want to write." It offers itself, as half a conversation, to all who want to make anything—anything but money.

In manuscript it has been read by a fellow who is running a power press, by an artist in housing and city planning, by a young writer, by a master of the graphic arts (and secretly much more), by a code clerk in the Office of Strategic Services, by a most imaginative grandmother, and by the founder of a clinic that is rectifying a grave physiological defect the existence and nature of which he discovered.

The last of these readers, one of the soundest of composers of fact and possibility, suggested division into two parts: Forming Your Meaning for Yourself, and Communicating the Meaning You Have Made. The first part, ending at Chapter 23, is for the painter, he says, or the musician or anyone who desires to make a form that mediates between the insufficient formed and the universal flux.

Well, if this is a composition you can't leave out some without altering its nature in every part. The ingredients all affect each other; all affect the whole. But lay it down whenever you feel inclined; where you stop will scarcely show in the composition of the future.

TABLE OF CONTENTS

Contents

Indirections

I

Nobody can tell you how to write

No MATTER how many good writers you have read, you never can anticipate a new one. The good ones start off from a tradition; they do not follow one.

And yet the significance of a writer is in the unpredictable pattern made by the opposing pull and tug: the pull of established practice and the tug of wayward impulse. If he varies from the long familiar and the now prevailing ways of other writers in every turn and twist, he cuts himself off from understanding. Besides, the very deepest motive that drives him to write is the lonely craving to be in touch with other people, without giving up his other main desires or his special sense of things.

Nobody can tell you how to write. But why not see what happens in your mind when exposed to some meditations of a friend of many writers?

II

The start-off

FIRST, we may as well get it out into the open that one of the springboards of writing is ambition. It is all very well to say that some people want to be writers, some want to write. Truth is in that statement. But writers are not exempt from human foibles like vanity; if they were they

[3

couldn't write for those of us who have the foibles. Call fame, if you like, what Milton called it, "the last infirmity of noble mind"; the large-souled, serene writers, with all but never-failing sense of humor, want to leave imprints. They may honestly prefer to live and let live, hate to be controlled and not ask to control others. But they like the subtler form of power, subtler and longer-lasting: influence. Everyone who has something to say wants readers and an effect on readers, and that means wanting to be a writer. The difference is that he will not give up what he means for the sake of being one.

We often hear of "the golden complex" and are told that poetry sought to make up for Byron's malformed foot and Pope's pint size. If we could do all we should like to, we should spend our energy without writing. Writers are not all grossly lacking, however, nor manifest incompetents in less specialized activities. No denying that many are. And if they are, it is so much gain in the economy of human value that they find, in using words, a way to even up. But writers have a good deal of energy, great writers, great natural force. Thoreau calls attention to the wide-ranging man of action, Sir Walter Raleigh, who wrote good things in prison. He says that the good writer may always be a captive knight, one who would have put his meaning into doing if he hadn't been, in some way, locked up. The best writing is like an act. It is an act that time or position forces into temporary suspension. The overt material effect may be a long time or a long way off, and it may be dispersed in many times and places, but if the writing is, in enough ways, good enough it will produce material effects.

Imitation cannot be passed over. One of the least imitative poets divulges that he first wrote a poem because he read a poem on the school blackboard and suddenly thought, "I could do that." In everything we learn to do there is emulation. But if we make good on our imitation we soon begin to try wrinkles of our own. Possibilities suddenly appear, as chickadees and juncoes do when seeds are scattered on the snow.

But, though ambition often provides some of the stimulus, and emulation sometimes supplies both incentive and a pattern to diverge from, there has to be something to say. One way the writer gets a theme is by feeling annoyed at attitudes that take too much for granted and suppositions that ignore differences. He knows there is more to life than glib assumptions take account of, and, for a while, he goes around irked by others' blindness, and a wild craving grows to make them see. All at once he witnesses some small event, recalls some person or has a situation occur to him, in which the ignored reality cannot be missed. He starts to write.

He humps himself to get the story told in such a way that no one can fail to see the little difference. At the same time he has to make sure that what everybody knows is in it too. He mustn't put the reader on his guard. The reader must be a discoverer. If only one reader might come round and say, "You know I was wondering. It just came to me." When you have made a reader wonder until a new realization comes to him you have done what you started out to do.

Delight you have experienced has as much to do with starting off to write as being irked. It makes great efforts seem worth while.

Masefield says, "The days that make us happy make us wise." On those days we probably don't write. But we keep from them a sureness. We never lose the knowledge that floods to our darkest hollows of something wonderful and real. The memory of what was too good, almost, to be true, yet really there and solid—that vibrates in our tissues. That nerves us for the preliminary doubting and for the destruction that we risk when we compose.

But don't expect to write well about the love affair that you are in the midst of, or have just mailed a letter to break off. One principal figure in that situation you can't see. At least one. Probably two. You are "involved." You don't surround it. You suffer or you triumph; you do not comprehend.

Later, all those feelings will become your knowledge. They will be of your knowledge and your wisdom when they no longer possess you. Your subject must be something you possess and can move all the way around. The former feelings that come together in your subject may include the most glorious or devastating that you ever had. And you will re-experience them. But you must emotionally enclose and dominate them. You have to know how to take things before you can find out what to make of them. You have to make a little of your life of them before you can make stories.

You will therefore respect experience more than you do ideas about experience. And the unfolding of your poem or story will have surprise for you before it has it for your reader. You will not force memories into a fixed design. For design in writing, the same as design in bug or tree, river course or mountain range, has time as one component. It defines itself, adapts itself, and changes as it grows and goes. You will welcome unexpected happy thoughts; possibilities will unpredictably disclose themselves; some of the little branches of your main idea will be nipped off as wasteful suckers; and by composing you will achieve design.

III

From feelings

WRITERS like Chaucer, Ben Jonson, Hardy are manifestly as far from hysterical as human beings can well be. And, in general, good writers are not flighty or obviously excitable. They are not "emotional people"; not as those who care little about words say "emotional." And yet the capacity to feel is one gift you must conserve and cherish if you want to be a writer. To feel intensely, sharply, exquisitely, variously, and far beyond the periphery of your private skin. To feel many kinds of feeling, and, more important still, not to check or muffle feelings but to feel them to the limit. Including ugly, dangerous, and extremely painful feelings.

But what I have said can easily mislead. When I say "must" I do not recommend trying to have violent feelings; I do not recommend straining for intensity; I do not mean that there is an obligation. The point is that writers get their power from the much that they have felt, and they get their subject matter from perceptions made vivid by emotion.

Doubtless, cold-blooded men like T. S. Eliot can write and have things to write about. They have had with sharpness the feelings of the cold-blooded: disappointment, disgust, ennui, loneliness, resentment, shock, generalized melancholy, fear, acute pain at discords and ironic clashes, mild pleasure in elegance and rightness, and a cool religious awe. By fidelity to feelings such as those and the patient and persistent development of the skills requisite to use them, T. S. Eliot has established a deep kinship with many of the thin-blooded of our time. And because many of the thin-blooded turn to literature and other men's ideas he has become the most conspicuous spokesman of men of brain who can't love living.

Ralph Waldo Emerson confessed to his Journal, about the time he went to Harvard, that he found himself deficient in animal spirits. He, too, failed to feel some of the normal human feelings at full strength. That did not prevent him from writing some of the best poems of the nineteenth century, or from being one of the greatest influences, through writing, that America has produced. You are not cut off from being a writer because you don't have all the human feelings in full strength.

But the writer who has seemed the greatest of all to the largest number of playgoers and readers in the last four and a half centuries is Shakespeare; and the deepest reason why so many people have genuinely liked his plays and poems and been influenced by him is that he had fully felt so many emotions. Large and little private feelings that make us difficult for people to understand find sympathetic understanding in the plays. And the most unlike among us discover in Shakespeare someone who understands. With the old yearning to be known and liked for what we are a little eased, we lend ourselves to him, as we read, and come to sympathize in turn with those who to us have seemed different and strange.

The wideness of his feelings and his fair expression of opposite feelings make thoughtful people say that Shakespeare had no philosophy. But if, by philosophy, we meant an organic response to the whole of life, he was about our best philosopher. He always approached, as a variable approaches a limit, the reconcilement of all his feelings. That is greatness.

But if you are capable of relatively few feelings but let yourself really have those few, you may achieve a clearness and a distinctness that will give your writings a fine and definite appeal. You may be a good writer with a small, select audience, and you may be assigned to all the students in a distant country to be studied, two centuries after you are dead, like Gray of the Elegy.

Contrariwise, if you feel more variously, with Tom, Dick, and Harry, and yet intensely too, and sharply, some fear or caution may so dominate your other feelings that, though everybody likes you, your vision, like Mark Twain's, will be a little skewed. In trying to bring home all your gains, you may drop some parcels because your arms are overfull.

And so, if advice could be wisely taken, the advice would be: feel all you have it in you to feel, up to the limit of your ability to make all the feelings correlate. But how are you to know? You probably will feel as you feel like feeling, regardless of advice.

Well, cherish your sensibility. And don't be fooled by what solemn people will say to you about discipline. If you want to write, take the discipline that is too exacting for the solemn and the timid: the discipline of pulling together some character and some meaning from the play of all the feelings. God knows, the feelings will check each other. If you love someone enough you won't kill him, no matter how angry at him you may be. The more feelings you have, the more serene you may finally become, because of the intricate balances and composings that your feelings will set up. On the contrary, of course, you may go crazy. But my bet is that you would, if that is the way your nerves behave, have gone crazy the other way from choking back emotion. Or else you would have stunted yourself into vacuity.

Caring for other people and wanting to be liked are most important and universal feelings. Do not feign pride that you are indifferent, or trifle with the hope that if you are wild you will turn out to be a Rimbaud. Of all the kinds of fools, and each of us is some kind, he was one of the most wasteful. Instead of collecting himself and all his feelings, Rimbaud seems to have successfully repressed several normal feelings. He does not illustrate the achievement of a spiritual design through the free play of all the emotions natural to him. Not many people do. But as the fullest human maturity is approached it is approached that way.

What passes for maturity will not suffice for a writer. And, no matter how young you are, it is not too soon for you to face the imaginative way. What passes for maturity is sunk into, by letting other genuine desires and embarrassing emotions be overridden by the desire to have peace now. The desire for peace is a central desire in all of us. And the great serenity is a peace that passeth understanding. For nearly all of us, all our lives, full composure, from the achieved composition of all our emotions, is far off. No one completely attains it while actively alive. But there are substitutes. All are fakes. One of the recurrent themes of writing is spurious maturity. Think of Prince Albert in Strachey's *Queen Victoria* or Richard Feverel's father or Polonius.

If security, high grades, reputation, a sure job, doing what is expected, avoiding trouble, or safety in any form becomes your most effectual desire, then you will accept discipline of the compromise variety; then you will be almost mature by the time you graduate from college. Soon you will cease growing, with a brief interlude of growth when you are in love. But, unless love is strong enough to put security forever in the second place, the growth and the love will be soon over. When you have settled in a job that denies desires you had fondly supposed were strong, then you will subside, with a fatal finality that nothing but a cataclysm is likely to disturb, into compromise maturity.

Even then you can be a writer. But not a good one. Your imagination will quietly atrophy.

Imaginative maturing is dangerous and all but impossibly difficult. But I call to witness all the best writers you have loved and laughed with and Lewis Carroll and Molière; writers you have loved and felt strong with and Tolstoy and Hemingway; writers you have loved and loved life with and Cervantes and Robert Frost; and writers you have loved and faced mystery with and Dostoevsky and Herman Melville; and all the wisest and most serene: that the hard way is the way of most fun, of most joy, and of meaning.

Should you come to see for yourself that security cannot be first, necessary as it always is for close second to any main desire, you will not need to be warned that even love must not induce you to force or feign a feeling. You will fear beyond all other fears any trifling with emotion. You will not express feelings because they are nice feelings that you want to be sure to have. You will not try to have them until you just naturally do. And you won't gush. For all the other feelings you have had and that matter to you will increasingly co-operate to tone each new feeling, modulate it, give it clarity and form.

And because you have all sorts of feelings and you have been moved so totally that you cannot be superficially swept, you will not get rigid with your emotions. Instead, let us hope, you will be poised for fun.

IV

For fun

TOP ACCOMPLISHMENT is reached when we care a lot and still have fun. That goes for business, love-making, politics, and housekeeping, apparently even war. And you must have seen how true it is of writing. Far from being a function of frivolity or indifference, grand fun has to do with guts. With confidence, complete commitment, and a kind of fatal preference for the slim chance.

Roosevelt and Churchill in the late war illustrate. Few men in history have been under such tremendous responsibility. Neither was insensitive or unaware. Yet both were having fun. In that gusto and mischievousness the people of the allies had confidence. Their honest chuckles shook rivets from the machine of the new order. We had what the war required because even in jeopardy we could afford a little fun.

Democracy and art both gamble on order not established but in the making.

Writing, when it is more than reporting or the working of old tricks, is exacting and yet fun. Writers like Joseph Conrad attempt the all but impossible. And Conrad said that writing was torture. But if you read any of his novels or short stories a second time you will sense that he enjoyed the struggle. You will see him maneuvering his ship into the wind. You will see him involving his narrative in the separate recitals of several observers, and his reader in the necessity of checking and comparing, as in *Lord Jim* or *Chance;* he is spreading all the sail the ship will carry. You will see him getting in another layer of reality, to make his story look the way experience looked to him, and making the reader feel that the victory in *Victory* was a real one even though with it came the loss of life; Conrad is loading his ship up to the safety limit. For he finds the significance in the struggle, and the more typhoons and immeasurable expanses of seductive, treacherous calm he steers you into, "to make you see," the more of his kind of fun he has.

Writers like Conrad who strive to make you feel the beauty and the mystery and challenge of responsible living never speak of "the writing game." The phrase suggests a swindle. And their kind of writing is no racket. Yet writing has points of likeness to a game. You play your best and have most fun when you have to use your head all the time, put all you have into every play, and keep taking chances. You find that you can make strokes and gets that you didn't know you had mastered. And as your skill increases you like to multiply the handicaps and hazards. Most similar of all is the dependence of success on your ability to induce the other fellow to play the game your way.

What a lifetime of high jinks Bernard Shaw has managed, cajoling myriads of people into supposedly "dismal" realms of politics and economics or lofty ones of ethics and aesthetics, and frisking away their formulas and jargon and making them take new looks.

Why do people who are not required to and who have no gowned and vested interest keep on reading *Gulliver's Travels* in spite of the savageness of Swift's indignation? Because grave truths generally kept dark are made buoyant by Swift's Lilliputian chuckles and Brobdingnagian laughs.

It is a waste to take on more gravity than you can develop the spiritual levity to have fun with. When Matthew Arnold forsook poetry, like "The Forsaken Merman," and buried part of his life, he began cultivating his own second best and perpetrated an injury upon the literary world. He gave up the struggle to digest the venom of his spleen and so toughen his resistance to the slings and arrows of outrageous fortune; his sense of humor stopped developing, and he sadly satisfied himself with wit. Though he still had wry fun, heavily teasing bishops and industrialists and self-righteously exposing the philistines, his high seriousness became high hat; the fun became a vestige, like the grin, in *Alice in Wonderland,* of the disappeared Cheshire cat. And "culture," after Matthew Arnold, was too often a remnant not particularly saving: a fixed smile, up a tree.

"Culture," that we lack the skill to keep in daily action frightens some of us so that seriousness breaks apart from fun. And we get pompous and important, cherishing so tenderly our fractured funny bone. But before we write our best the break between fun and serious feeling will have to knit.

V

With sensations

WORDSWORTH had fun in the days before he felt too guilty about his own daughter and prayed to hear the voice of God's "stern daughter," Duty. Much of his fun came in turning from generalized reason, generalized nature, and generalized man to the celandine, the green linnet, the daffodils, and to casually met, vividly sensed men, like the leech-gatherer and Michael, and then exhibiting the broad truths and thoughts that lie too deep for tears, gradually suggested by his small sensations.

Part of the fun for Robert Frost is in caring so much for facts that he almost seems, sometimes, to care only for facts. It is a big risk he takes; a lot of learned and some gifted people see no further than his particulars, and fail to pierce to the significance of which the particular facts and his way of taking them are the signs. But in our lives the meaning is important and exciting in each particular instance, if it is important and moving in general. Any universal that *all* the instances suggest must be implicit amid the confused details of each single instance. If we miss the significance that subtly lurks in simple, sharply sensed experiences, any general ideas we may treat solemnly stay sterile. That is why Frost's risk is worth running. What he does is start people's imaginations so that they can better discover and enjoy their own actual experiences when no poet is by to provide the imagination.

If you like living, where you happen to be and day by day, you will care for your sensations. Your caring for and about them reveals, and co-operates in establishing, their meaning. You will use them when you write.

The books about composition agree on the importance of observing. But some might make you think you should collect with nets, cork sheets, and cyanide. You had better not get conscientious. Get impressions in your own unsystematic way. Any solemnly-noted-down sensation that lacks mysterious memorableness for you may self-importantly seduce you to force it into what you write. More likely than not it will be a Christmas tree fandangle on a blossoming apple tree.

Your sensations will hook up with your enthusiasms and affections if you do not interfere. Some positive, with pleasure, some negative, with disgust, horror, pain. Just go ahead about your necessities and your untutored inclination, not belittling your casual, crude experience, and, above all, not letting anyone start you trying to be what you are not, lest you become wastefully self-conscious and your senses get benumbed. Many of the sights, sounds, tastes, many of the smells and sensations of smooth and rough that you can with words make vivid and suggestive came to you intense, because an emotion sensitized you at the time. Such experiences are livelier than any for which you peep and botanize.

When you look over what you write, if you find yourself employing sniffs of smell and flicks of touch and interior sensations of the heft and hang that have not appeared in Tennyson, Henry James, or Thomas Wolfe, be glad. But do not bar the mention of the cool, smooth crispness of clean pillow slips because the sensation has been written of before. There can be no rhythm of interesting surprises when everything seems strange.

Only, be sure that admiration for another author is not the main selective magnet that picks out the shapes and textures, moves and colors that you use. What you pick up in passing and out of the corner of your eye is sure to be authentic. Sensations received long before it crossed your mind that you might write will revive more sharply than any that shared your attention with thoughts of literary use. The things you experience as literary material, putting half your mind on how you will use them, are not experiences as they come to Jack and Jill. Less respected than the literature they resemble, they lack vitality to stir the senses, once they are flattened by a printing press. And what you want to make us think of mainly is our own sensuous experience, less sharply sensed and never perceived in the relation-pattern that makes it meaningful for you.

Any natural sensations may be important. Don't do anything about them. Just keep your nerves from getting dull and let them happen; use them when they signify.

VI

Inducing others to play

WE CAN ALL meet on sensations. Some of us have most of them rather dimly because of natural defect or because we are preoccupied with what other people think of us. They may be dim because we're always busy making sense of something that has happened, because our work or play engrosses our attention, or, at worst, because we have lost our appetite for life. But we all have sensations. Dim or sharp, the middle register of sights, sounds, and the other primary sensations is common to us all, and when a writer revives and combines our memories of them private fears are seldom roused or apple carts of compromise upset.

When we have something to say to people whose fears and loyalties are partly different from ours—and that means nearly everyone—we can, therefore, do it best by a reach below their prejudices and compromises to stir their memories of unconventionalized sensation into play. That is the beginning.

The lucky turn you give the opening sentence may make your reader cock his ear. A little later you may start an uncompleted sniff. Then you call up three or four little sights he pleasurably remembers and get him piecing them together to imagine something new. His imagination is playing under your control.

And soon, with no emotional language and no opinionating, you are summoning his feelings. For sensations soon arouse emotions. Your feelings are selecting his sensations and combining them; you are dislodging his components, from buried nooks and surface patches, to join up in ways never his before.

Once he is interested enough you can give your own feelings more play. He'll stay with you if you keep his sense memories active and win his help with curiosity. You give him little satisfactions. And an unconscious hope grows in him that he will presently have all this in his control. You find ways to dangle that incentive, never letting him suspect.

You need have no qualms. You are trying to make his elements dance to your piping. But the way they hop and whirl, twine and join is, you hope, almost the way your own are doing as you write. The elements, you have in common. What comes into action in the interplay is as real as you can make it. And there is no coercion, only the interest you arouse and your charming way of saying things.

You never look on, of course, and describe the process to yourself. You don't think of taking your reader's imagination for your dancing bear. You are saying what you mean, telling a story that fascinates you, putting into words an experience, giving him a piece of your mind. You are showing something you have found out about conditions and possibilities of life. You are drawing inferences from kinds and kinks of human nature. You are entertaining him and implying, incidentally, something you believe, you are exciting commiseration for neglected people, or you are rousing admiration for a plucky fight. You are slyly lending out your eyes and insight. Or you're just having fun, seeing how much you can make things that delight and hurt you come to life.

But the writing act never stops with the typed or printed page. The completion is accomplished in another mind. And if that other mind comes back with, "Sure, sure.

You're dead right. A delightful piece of writing," then you have failed.

What you mean is never what anyone else means, exactly. And the only thing that makes you more than a drop in the common bucket, a particle of sand in the universal hourglass, is the interplay of your specialness with your commonness.

If you are to be a speck of yeast to aid the rising of lump man to potential man, if you are to be a minute participant in the maturing of civilization, you will function by waking to life uniqueness kin to yours, but not identical. As a writer you make your attempt by writing.

Knowing that your real effect is next to nothing, you try to move others. Move them. Not merely pat and tickle. Not merely give them some ephemeral "palps." You try to shake, stir, more fully mix their ingredients. You try to set them back and exercise the muscles that adjust their vision so that thereafter they are seeing with a sharper focus, from a more inclusive point of view.

Inflate them, and they will shrivel back like a dwindling blowfish when the water they are used to enters at their gills. Shove them and they will spring back like a sea snail when its sucking member is attached. What works is to modify the way they are put together, by winning their components for a moment to rearrange.

By inveigling your readers to play, their imaginations momentarily, incompletely matching yours, you solve the paradoxical dilemma in these true and contradictory familiar sayings: "Tell me something I don't know" and "You can't tell anybody anything he doesn't know." You do it by using what he already knows and cajoling him into setting this by that—this from strict category, that which he has never catalogued at all. And suddenly with his own half-forgotten knowledge, the familiar and the neglected, the ordered and the unsystematized, he has made a pattern that becomes his knowledge, but that up to now he didn't possess at all. "I never realized," he says.

All old stuff, what he uses is; but something new under the sun comes into being, something new in his mind. Slight of course, immeasurable, but creation.

VII

According to the rules

ANYTHING so much like a violation as manipulating another man's imagination requires all the tranquilizing you can administer. Your reader has to be assured that he is on familiar ground. The more so, the more daring your intention.

Even though you are, in a sense, endeavoring to finagle him into learning a new language, you must all the more give him the safe feeling that this is the sort of thing he can take in stride.

You are certain of the freshness of your meaning, and you slyly go more than halfway to meet him on familiar ground. You are conventional for the sake of originality. Not your originality. You use convention for the sake of numbing his reluctance to be a little original himself.

Even without such serpentine motives, any writer wants to be read. And so all use sentences and paragraphs, punctuation, and structures and arrangements that seem law-abiding; all observe the usage of our temperament-molded, history-determined native speech.

Most of that usage we take in as we do "the air we

breathe" and our mother's milk. Talking plays a much greater part than reading. Listening, first, then talking. For, without thinking about it, we try from babyhood for effects in speech that we have seen produced in others, had produced in ourselves. When we fail we listen again and modify our next attempt. And from earliest childhood we get a glow of corroboration at the sought-for twinkle, the frown, the shudder.

We look all the time for ways of speaking that have the quick, the subtle, or the bold effect of blows, menaces, flaunts, stamps, whistles, hisses, groans, gasps, growls, shrugs, Bronx cheers, winks, smiles, snuggles, pats, caresses. We listen for word and tone combinations that are like such acts as slamming doors, looking back through windows, swinging an ax to cut out a substantial chip, pulling up a bucket from a deep, dark well. We find speech ways that glide, that soar, that sweep, that come to a dead stop. We hunt, like well-trained hounds, the scent of language forms that leap, run, swim, climb. We gather phrases that can crinkle, wrinkle, flap, and bounce. We stalk turns and sinuous inflections that curve in upon themselves, that make a long sure trajectory. We corral unbroken idioms that weave, that rear up, prance, and gambol. We listen for all the ways that words can match the involutions, convolutions, evolutions of man's behavior.

And when we who attempt to write are reading, we keep many planes and tangents of attention. On one or two planes we are continuously learning all the modes, forms, tricks, devices, and learning when they are appropriate and what exactly each one does.

We get to know our language, better and better, and always more intricately and subtly. We get to love it. And we have to be on guard lest interest in language ever crowd out interest in things, changes and relations, actions, people. The possibilities of speech matter superlatively to a writer. Yet the writing is precious and of no value if meanings grasped by readers do not always matter more.

You are always trying to change the game, whatever the game happens to be in which you are at the moment interested; for that very reason you do your playing and your magic-working regardful of the rules. You compensate for preferring form to formula by employing some formulas.

Playing according to the writing rules is, therefore, not compromise; it is creative resolution. If you have enough in balance in you of all that constitutes a gracious, forceful human being, you will be all the time affecting usage. You will be helping make new rules.

VIII

To take the vapor threads of possibility that run up from earth to heaven and weave them with the warp of days

EXPERIENCES, conventions, and desires. From them we make our lives. Within the confine of our inborn limitations and our circumstances. And with experiences, conventions, and desires we write.

The word "ideals" is used in such a statement more often than the word "desires." But it has such various meanings that the speaker and the hearer often fail to mean the same. The word is liked for its vague loftiness, its noncommittal suitability to extend in high-pitched wishes and profuse professions and to contract, like an accordion, to cautious soundlessness. Its commonest use, even with those who have studied Oriental classics, Plato, Berkeley, is in opposition to "practical." What would be fine if there were no hampering conditions but cannot work in crude, thwarting actual circumstances is "ideal."

We will say "desire." And we will mean sex desire, the desire for food, the desire for security, the desire for variety, the desire for recognition and the desire for response, and other desires sprung from those and charged with their voltage. So, we shall include all genuine spiritual forces, ignoring for the present ideal veils and sops or patterns in the sky that no more determine action than Cassiopeia's Chair.

But desires do give rise to daydreams. Complex desires, even if sexual desire is their core, often cannot be directly or completely realized in acts. Yet the daydream need not be a wasteful substitute. It can be an unsystematic exploration of a way. It can go beyond the state of fancying unrestricted satisfaction. Convincing force is shown when the dream is brought down to relevant memories of action, the unrealizable components ruthlessly abandoned, the practicable components put together for a test, and a leap taken toward the not yet demonstrated but dream-discovered possibility. That "imaginative leap," which Professor Whitehead defined a few years ago in philosophic terms, is so much the one thing needful for nonmaterial growth that of course it has been taken countless times.

It is always taken in creation. And the writer, or any genuine artist, takes it many times in living for once he takes it pen in hand. The best writers dream dreams and, like Joseph as shown by Thomas Mann, they find in dreams realizable possibilities, and then go on to realize them. If part, still, of the dream has to be discarded, they discard it. But they invariably include what the timidly practical would not dare attempt.

They value the daydream. But they do not value it more than life. They value it for life. And if they can realize some of it, no matter if the dream is left a thing of shreds and patches. They can dream again. Airy nothings demonstrate their worth when, and only when, they get a local habitation and a name. The writer who is imaginative in more than words ravels threads of possibility from the dream the sun draws up from sweat and tears in his depressions. He selects and winds those ravelings that though tenuous are tough and weaves them into the warp of necessity and fact.

There are sunset colorings to which an imaginative person can only lift his eyes. They keep him humble and aspiring. He is fortunate if the discrepancy between dream and possibility also deepens his sense of humor.

For when his desire is strong enough to force the skyey web apart, the writer always meets resistance. The timid want dreams left intact. They want facts and what they call ideals kept apart. And though the writer's patience, deviousness, and humanness may eventually get around repudiation, his patterns woven in the warp of days are generally labeled as "ideal" and used as ornamental hangings well away from muddy boots.

But the mischievous attempt goes on. The enterprise will never stop. Weaving possibilities into (a little) practice is more effectual and more fun than gazing at supernal radiance until the rats begin to gnaw.

IX

Being independent yet belonging

GETTING OTHERS to take seriously the fabric that your imagination weaves from inherited predisposition, experience, and the possibilities disentangled from your dreams takes confidence. Yet very likely you are shy and modest. You let others go their ways and only ask to be allowed to go your own. You like affection and companionship, however; you want to feel that you belong. What you work for is fuller, less embarrassed give-and-take.

No one has to read the things you write. Those who read are not obliged to accept your image of reality. You outdo yourself to win not subservience but confidence, and convince them, if you can, of the realness and the worth of things that interest you. You summon all your skill and all your sympathy to secure their brief assent to your design. Unconsciously you warm and stir them, if animated words and exciting scenes will do it, so that their angles, straightnesses, and set curves flow and fit the shape of your story or your poem.

Putting things together with you, while they read, may render a few readers less rigid and inert. Then you have done your lucky little toward an order which allows some give-and-take. By your intrepidity you have given your responsive readers a start toward being more actively responsible and more nearly free. You have stimulated the growth that you desire for yourself: becoming independent while more neighborly belonging.

To acquire such power you need, more than common

strength of the common senses, full possession of common impulses and such clarity of common knowledge that the knowledge is surpassing. For imagination is not a magic attribute useless in practical behavior but inexplicably employed by geniuses. It is energy finding ways to put together the stuff of common life—the stuff of common life and the stuff of dreams that we dream in the daytime because our activity gets caught against a snag or runs up against a wall. Imagining is acting things to shapes that the things and our desires suggest; it is discovering further ways to act when immediate action is stopped; and it is acting those dreamed ways into our whole performance, once we have pulled them apart from vain, deceptive wish.

Few of us, however, have those requisites complete. Few who eventually write well can function without obstruction and delay. The discipline of many tries, encouraged by a little success, hardens the spiritual fibers to separate the practicable possibility from the figment of mere wish. It is a taxing growth. And, knowing writers, we know there is no standardized equipment that all possess.

Meanwhile we seek our independence and retain our hankering to belong. Gradually we sever the umbilical cord of family, cut the apron string thread by thread. Each act of risky independence is a cut. And I was going to say the severing is easier if parents have lives, still, of their own and the wisdom to prefer a maturing son or daughter to the no-longer-flattering infant bond. But what I was going to say is too facile. Sometimes, when parents encourage independence, what happens is but a stretching of the cord. And sometimes the violent snatch and tear is best.

Whichever way, the severance has to happen. And, however devastating, the belonging cannot cease. You will always be the son or daughter of the hereditary chromosomes. You will always be the creature once surrounded by a certain nest. You will always be the one who had your particular grandparents, lived so many years in a certain special psychic atmosphere, and had a unique set of pressures to yield to and resist. Breeding, bringing up or being left to come up, and the composite interplay of family remain determinants of you. And usually you will cherish, even though you may regret; you will be glad of the fostering that was partly crippling, while you see how this trait got overdeveloped, that gnarl got fixed in your main trunk. Do what we may about it, to the family we belong.

So do we to an early segment or segments of the earth. The small village undertaker's storehouse inside the parsonage picket fence, into the windows of which I peeped, stretched up on tips of toes, is part of me. So are the long funeral processions breaking into a trot at the foot of the hill where I sat watching, under Grandpa's chestnut tree. And so are Grandma's saintly smiles at her desk, her hired girl's doughnuts, songs, and friendly stories, her flowerbeds, pears, and flowering shrubs. And picking field strawberries with the kids and pulling chickweed, by myself, while cheers resounded from the baseball game.

The lawn you mowed in August when the grass had grown a foot is in your arms, back, memory. And so is the mountain where you climbed the ledges and sought out robber caves. Aunt Emma's clicking teeth are part and her saying, when you tipped over the paint table by the tall ice chest, "Never use anything except for the purpose for which it was made!" Ice storms are part, and fires that you faced into the blizzard through a foot of snow to reach; extricating your car, stuck in foot-deep mud, is part, and the flush that went all over you when an otherwise forgotten girl went by your desk in the eighth grade.

You belong where you have lived, and most where you got your first millions of impressions of the world.

Words and phrases, also, with which you register your experiences and imitate, report, and comment, the turns of speech, accents, pronunciations, rhythms, drawls, and clippings bind you to your country and your region. Old sayings, proverbs, gags and anecdotes that carry them, the constant references to men and women who made history, national or local, and the deeds that they performed: all these run into you and through you and cause you to belong.

It is a good, loose, almost free belonging and the boundaries are not exact. Some belong to more parts of America than others and, by the same token, do not belong so fully to New England or the West. Naturally, the more we belong, the less the specialness we are part of seems anything to notice. A little detachment makes us look and listen to the land where we belong; our own becomes a thing to write about when we are sick for home.

One more kind of membership is complicating but desirable for a writer. Seeing all the pain it costs to wives and children, one of those children grown up sometimes declares the artist should not marry. And surely no one who has not yet brought to the end of life a lasting love affair is free to insist that writers ought to marry. But this much can be seen: the more the writer avoids and seeks exemption, the less he speaks "as one having authority" to those unexempt. Besides, you know a different and lesser love if your desires and affections do not involve you in the full cycle of sex experience: babies, quarrels, mutual influence and irritation, accommodation, and seeing each other through crises, great and small. So enduring and enjoying, you become a little solider and richer, a little mellower and tougher, a little more aware in nerve and tissue of the way things are.

If children interfere with writing, that is dreadful; yes, but seeing a child grow can provide more valid sights and insights than months of reading clinical and psychological reports. Especially if the child is yours and forces you to grow and change with him. A writer should be subject to all kinds of weather; not live always air-conditioned. If he takes from his family more than some of them can realize that he gives, that is bad: but he may give proportionately to those who read his work. As long as the marrying comes from desire and affection on both sides, let's call it good.

Those are the memberships for a writer: in humanity, in the family he is born in and the family with his mate, and in the large, loose fellowship and attachment of his country.

The writers who stay sensitive and who have most in common with us all let us forget their class. They look too penetratingly to see men as tailored tweed, ordinary suit, or overalls. They can't and don't ignore the part of circumstance in shaping us. But they find likeness among men from all the income brackets and more important differences among the members of a club.

This doesn't mean: sedulously cultivate your type. Types, too, are rigid. Those who think of men and women by types slight the differences that give the likeness interest. To join the artist type, yourself, is deadly. If you want to see, feel, realize, never missing flair or flavor, you will steadfastly remain man or woman more than writer.

The difference between the artist and the craftsman is that the artist takes that chance. The craftsman belongs to his craft; the artist does not. The artist doesn't standardize himself, his process, or his product. He quietly but confidently keeps free up to the fatal moment. The fatal moment in composition is when the last stroke of work is done. The fatal moment with his technique is when he finishes his last creative work. And the fatal moment with himself is when he dies.

Thomas Mann has written stories showing how one

gives up being a warm, participating human being, in re-
turn for the detachment that enables him to take a far
perspective. But it is not necesssary to be inhuman to avert
the astigmatism that blurs eyes always on the clock. And
in Mann's more recent books he seems to question the
Latin Quarter heresy, that the artist is both cut off and
privileged. He has included among dilemmas that it is the
artist's task to take by both the horns, the dilemma of
being responsible, limited, and involved man and, at the
same time, free-seeing, comprehending artist, the dilemma
of detachment with attachment.

Great artists belong to life and so does their art. Their
greatness shows in the dilemmas they resolve. In a future
book I hope to show that one writer of our day, because
he belongs with long, entwined filaments to humanity, his
family, and his country and because he commits himself
so little to organizations set by clock and calendar, has
attachment in detachment, detachment in attachment. He
belongs, while very much alive, to both time and timeless-
ness.

Dogmas and doctrines the writer needs to understand.
They help him to know people, history, and his time. But
he can belong to his world, his country, and his home
without being either dogmatist or doctrinaire. And his
imagination begins to wither as soon as he is either one.

For, just as living people bulge over and concave within
the finest-fitting types, experience breaks the shape of any
formula. You have to confine your experience, as you confine water in pipe or pail, to keep it even temporarily true
to formula. Reality takes and gives form changingly, as
rain does in drops, brooks, rivers, lakes, and seas; as it does
in wearing mountains down to buttes and mesas. And
since there is no final form — unless it is a work of art no
longer boldly looked at and so become mere object of sale

and reverence—the wisest writer commits himself to no formulas.

A formula rapidly becomes a convenience of the status. It is useful and necessary, as pipes and pails are to take water to the bathroom and to fires. But formula is the foe of form. And the writer never quite submits to one, but makes any that he touches fuse and flow, with new ingredients, to new form.

Writers are affected by literature, though they do not belong to it; only their completed and successful works belong. Tradition is at their back, however. And one important realization that good writers derive from literature and history is that the world is always going to the bow-wows but never goes. Their reading in great authors prepares them for a world that is sad and funny, adventurous and treacherous, and tragic when it isn't comic.

The great ones seem to say it is a good world, to which the writer, staying independent, can belong.

X

Using symbols to keep in touch

Do you often say, "I'll take my chances"? Or do you more often say, "I just want to know what to expect"? Is what you ask from life each day your chance? Or is it certainty?

How you answer depends on and indicates your temperament. Able writers belong to both groups. Burke was for certainty, Fielding for his chance. Among chance-takers were Euripides, Plato, Shakespeare, Keats, Browning, Melville. Among those bent on certainties were Aeschylus, Aristotle, Milton, Wordsworth, Arnold, Henry James. Good writers, like all of us who are not one-sided, have both desires. And some, like Chaucer, Goethe, and Tolstoy, it would be possible to claim for either group.

Of moderns, I would put James Joyce among the certainty-seekers. And James Stephens, for the sake of a few good poems, I would name among the takers of chances. Proust was a most pertinacious seeker of certainties. And so was the phosphorescent Rilke. And so was Virginia Woolf. And so are Tate, Eliot, Ransom, and Horace Gregory. Among contemporary chance-takers are Bernard Shaw, Wallace Stevens, Hemingway, since he recovered the use of his right as well as his left wing, Frost, Katherine Porter, Jessamyn West, and Arthur Koestler.

This temperamental difference will have much to do with which kind of symbols you use in writing. If your confidence is in yourself and your ability to cope with things as they come up, no matter how unfamiliarly they arrange themselves, then you will find your symbols in casual particulars.

If, instead, your confidence is in what you have learned from others, and in techniques you have acquired and assembled, you will prefer sterile and sanctified symbols, like the fish, the boarhound, the tower, and the chalice. Or you will invent a set of new code signs that those who care to read you will have to get from some follower of yours. Many literary symbols are as little related to concrete particulars as π in mathematics. They are meaningful only because of what you can learn that they are "equal to." If such symbols are your choice you will belong to the initiates; readers will gain an entry into an inner circle as they are taught or laboriously puzzle out. You may have expositors while you are alive. Professors will be glad of you; in your works they have "something to teach." You will contribute to the literature that is akin to the Sibylline Books. If your gifts are great enough you may become Past Grand Masters of the secret shrine, hierophants and hierarchs of the Rosicrucian Rose. Half the timid-serious minds of our day are prostrated before such writers. Prostrated. Nervous prostration from overwork and deficiency of nutriment.

As a chance-taker you are rather one of *hoi polloi*. Your work is likely to be stigmatized as "popular." Custodians of the higher taste will mistake your everydayness for triviality. They will attribute the exhilaration that people gradually get from you to the cheap tricks of the charlatan. You can smile at their failure in discernment. For the maturest, sanest artists, like charlatans, are chance-takers; they, also, care about the workings of the unintellectual mind. Their glory is an effectual performance, and, though masters of an intricate technique, they carefully conceal devices by which they carry out their feats. They always have something up their sleeves. And the best ones have a humorous wink. They baffle the solemn explainers. They lure the unspoiled.

As a chance-taker you set experience, here and now, above the intricacies of ancient lore, higher than Aristotle, Aquinas, Einstein, Marx, or Freud, higher, even, than the magnificence of art. Your so doing may blind the erudite. They know too little of life outside museums and libraries to respect your quiet fidelity to real sensations, real desires, real feelings, real relations, and to so much of tradition as concrete experience corroborates. If their too-trained perceptions overlook your passionate genuineness, they cannot co-operate in the act of enjoyably discovering wisdom. You may seem superficial, you may seem falsely simple, you may seem smug, you may seem an irresponsible acrobat; your symbols will not symbolize for them.

So be it. Both life and art remain for you adventure. You can learn to see the joke and go your way in patience, doggedly but not, tail between your legs, an underdog.

But what kind of symbols are those? "Doggedly" and "underdog"? Well, once they were casual and straight from perceived likeness. Now they can be used and understood as mere Morse code. You see no dog, smell no dog, hear no dog when I say "doggedly." Men say "underdog" who, if they saw two puppies playing, would turn away uninterested. They wouldn't notice that now one was underdog and now the other. Once a living metaphor, for most of us it is dead. (Now as we reconsider it, it comes to life.) My use of "tail between the legs" might revive it; only that expression, too, is used "figuratively" more than literally; so that dog, tail, and doggedness are overdomesticated.

Overdomesticated symbols are for short cuts; they take us in straight lines from point to point. Like shells that once sheltered, and grew with, living creatures, they are empty now and crushed to build highways. They suffice for uneventful transportation.

It would be quixotic to discard them. So would it to discard all symbols that only bookish people fully grasp. Crackling abandoned skin though the word "quixotic" is to those who have never liked and laughed at poor, enthusiastic Don Quixote, you will forgive a bookman's making that allusion when you read Cervantes' book. And yet we had all better write with symbols that have for all our readers living literal shape and motion. At best our descendants will probably keep on hearing of harps and shamrocks on Saint Patrick's Day after no Americans but scholars know the actual sham*rock* from the blarney stone.

It is one sort of fun to figure out what the doubloon that Ahab nailed to the mast in *Moby Dick* is equal to. It is pleasant to know what to think when we read "pylon" in a poem by Day Lewis. Exciting hours can be spent in guessing and discussing what Enitharmon stands for in a poem by William Blake. It would be wasteful to attack a sometimes wise, brave poet for his contributions to the higher wit-sharpening games.

But when we desire to get in touch with people who have no vanity about literary puzzles and know nothing of the phoenix, the roc, or the occult, rhapsodic Omm, when we desire to convince people that adventure, joy, and meaning are possible in plain lives, then we had better stay as close as print and words will let us to specific sense experience. We had better show by cases, reveal in instances. To let meanings emerge, as they once emerged for us, from realities physically experienced and then spiritually grasped is to help readers discover for themselves.

The most valid symbols are just plain samples. But it exacts great faith and self-effacement to set simple samples before us with such skill that all they represent eventually fills the reader's mind.

XI

Fixing meanings by interplay

FROM THE SMALLEST matter of punctuation to the largest notion of the universe the choice keeps offering itself: more certainty with loss of the changefulness of living or more life with the loss of facile clarity. And just as most of us would usually rather be in a snug, well-heated house with the newest appliances than in a southern Pacific jungle or in an open boat at sea, so some of us prefer definite fixing of the meaning of words and the new authoritative principles of communication. We want, to be sure, some liberality; we still want something left to the imagination. But we would rather acquire a system of semantics, trying to keep up with each new correction, than to be alone, first thing we know, with nothing but imagination to bind us to other men.

The attractions of the moving, changing world, however, usually distract the artist from intellectual systems. He is interested for a while, picks up a good deal, quickly rather than meticulously, and never trusts any explanation as he does experience. For a while his life moves back and forth between the ordered world of classic and current dogma-specialists and the dangerous, changeful world that is always grassing over roads and deflecting compass needles.

That vibration is not to be condemned in the young writer who has yet to find his way. He needs to keep connection with organized thought at least as much as potential readers who are busy reconverting, striking, controlling the atom bomb, and insuring peace. But it is too bad if he takes organized thought more trustingly than he takes organized business, religion, or politics.

How much you keep touch with the growing tip of life, where are also frosts and blight, depends on the stoutness of your stomach. The more you like life, the more you will keep returning to that point where no *ratio* is rational.

The more you are discouraged, your very impulses half congealed, the less you will gamble on that which is not fixed. And then the planners and explainers, with their floors above volcanoes and vast piers above the sea, will influence what you write and, still more, the way you write.

Over and over again in school and university you are confronted by opposite challenges. Men whose memories are more impressive than their bodies, or their ways with human beings, tell you to trust the intellect. They warn you to keep emotions leashed. They urge you to check, as at a bundle room, your natural impulses. Then you read Emerson, Whitman, Blake, and D. H. Lawrence, and maybe some of Rabelais; they suggest trusting your whole self. There is something frightening, possibly disgusting, in some of the lives or writings. They are described to you as "romantic," feverish, incompetent to face the facts. You are warned of wishful thinking, and taught vague scorn of sentimentality.

In your confusion you may begin to envy the grim dignity of the rationalists. You emulate those who disguise and deny their feelings. Who can wonder if you turn to dates and data? Who can wonder if you try to pile up blocks of knowledge, cut and dried? Who can wonder if you put your mind on structure, straining for dexterity with such forms and symbols as the coldest critics now impersonally praise?

But there is another way of taking the indeterminateness of things. It ought to be congenial to one who has had fun writing. And it ought to make his writing greater fun. Why not accept the fact of relativity? Suppose that both the observer and the thing observed "do move"; turn it to account. Many centuries ago Heraclitus made the assertion, "All things flow." And most great writers have implied that men are mutable and all things transitory. Yet all of them have demonstrated that there is, notwithstanding, form.

All things flow, but some things flow to form. And intent can be active in the form. As long as the form is vital it sets up a flow. May it not be that all things flow to form? May it not be that form flows to form, as in the ocean waves? May it not be that flow takes form to flow, as with the chromosomes? (You know the chromosomes determine your traits, yet some now latent in you flowed in from both streams of ancestry and will blend with another stream to flow on through your son.) If such is the way things seem to you, why not be willingly of the flow? Why not be a formative intention in the flux? Why not make your writing be a flow to form?

Did you ever hear of river drivers? They were men who guided logs down swollen springtime rivers to the lumber mills. They were of the flood, and the logs they rode were of it, too. But they put order in the watery wildness as it swept them on. And they had fun proportioned to the ever-present hazard. They poised on their spiked boots, with cant dogs in their hands. When a snag stopped a log and those rushing from behind rose over it and began to make a jam, the river drivers ran from log to log, leaping gaps of raging water. Where the pile-up was they heaved and pried, letting weight and current aid, and picked the jam apart.

Sometimes a single log started rolling with a driver, as if, in malicious mischief, it would toss him to the dark stream beneath the drive. With gloating hoots, the driver would run backwards, in one place, and force the log to float without a roll. At last thousands of feet of timber, guided by men swept upon and with them, reached the mill. And there a boom of logs, chained end to end in a long curve and made fast to the banks, held the timber flood for hours or days, a single form.

Something akin to that writers can attempt. Sometimes their poise and mastery wins other men to ride the flux of life with spirits that grow confident, as the flux, for them in turn, yields to their intent.

If you find that giving form to flow is what you see around you, in plant, animal, and planet, in history and in yourself; if you find that there is intention in a pine distinguishing it from a palm, and yet no single palm or pine has predetermined form, but grows to its design, then you will want your writing, too, to flow to form.

You will define by using. Your whole composition will indicate the way to take each paragraph. The whole composition and the including paragraph will show how to read the sentence. And all three will give the reference frame to the individual word, and each word act upon the meaning of its neighbors. There will be flow through all. The flow will gain momentum and inflection from the slightest syllable. And all will bring to pass the developing intention.

With such control you will carry on the interplay with readers, engaging their imaginations to compose with you, and, for the brief duration of your spell, flow to your form.

Of a temperament that craves certainty this is a lot to ask. But as soon as you have discovered for yourself that certainties must be created to be had, you might as well begin to learn to ride the flux and shape a little, as it flows, to your fluent but positive intent. Doing so you will have your times of loving the dangerous flood you ride and guide.

XII

For writing is a minor variant
of the universal process

IMAGINATION is our participation in continuing creation.*
Farmers, builders, housewives, both as homemakers and

---

* See Gertrude Stein's little essay on "Composition," which includes one of the best of philosophic formulas: "Everything is the composition and the time of the composition and the time in the composition."

mothers, business men, industrialists, and men in politics: all participate when they take a hand combining elements. So do trappers and mechanics, all who sense a possibility and achieve it with a rigged-up device. One by one and all together, purposely or not, all are composing constantly a developing design. All the arts, including writing, belong to the composition, and their small individual composing affects the human whole.

When Thomas Hardy writes a poem, "God's Education," he is giving responsive readers an experience from which they emerge encouraged to use imagination; they have the thought and feeling that by every generous and responsible imagination the intent of all creation may be rendered more alert. If Egdon Heath suggests indifference in the revolving aeons, through the perceptions and formed purposes of men may evolve the undiscoverable intent.

Or you may think, as most Christians have, that the intent is always there, leaving men to perceive and realize it, by putting their treasure in the kingdom of heaven and seeking God's kingdom first. (In the days of Jesus "the kingdom of heaven" was an adequate phrase for the dream from which he drew filaments of possibility to weave into his deeds.)

Either way, serious writers, like Glenway Wescott in America and E. M. Forster in England, no matter how the church may disapprove of them or they of the church, are revealers of creative possibility. They and all real ones minimize their office. The huge discrepancy between intention and accomplishment keeps good writers humble. It keeps them humorous. For sharing and possessing large intentions makes one either pompous, self-pitying, or humorous. Some of us show traces of all three.

That is not strange. This world may be in flux. But each of us soon finds that there are limitations. They are both around and in us. And frustration seems to be a constant. Most of us, after a few collisions and repulses, cease pushing limitations to their limits. We might collect ourselves after each rebuff and make our next lunge with more imagination. If we did, and of course the great ones often do, we might push our limits hard enough to know more clearly what they really are.

By concentrating all that is in us, and using it with increasing cunning, we discover what we are. It is so with writers who write five, ten, twenty years before they are recognized, and yet, instead of compromising, intensify their stuff. They get more and more composed as they continue with their composition.

They become proficient at recognizing their chances; they keep taking them for all that they are worth. And, though their material may be things as they actually are, their intention recognizes and their living tests possibilities that realism can leave out. In their limited creation they are always proving possibilities.

They are concerned with ultimates in spite of relativity. But, because they feel relations and accept experience as a composition, ultimates for them are not things last in time. Progress is not their metaphor. The life they make and the writing they do are not linear. They take in what they can of the things that their desires bring them up against, and they make something of all they really take. They make something rather spherical than prolonged, a microcosm, a little world.

And their ultimates, not measurable by time, are such things as elation, loneliness, and struggle; such things as necessity, hate and love, fun, grief, sympathy, and faith: such a thing as the joy and wonder of two minds creating a new, live realization together, in the air between them, but solid there for both to see and say, "It is not mine nor yours, but ours!" (The joy of a shared flash of insight is an ultimate, and sometimes it comes with one who never shares your serious large words.)

Ultimates run off tangent to the clock dial; they break the endless circle of hour and minute hands. They transgress boundaries of ownership and state. They influence the intention which makes of flux a form. And it is their indwelling presence in the world and in a poem that makes a composition that is not an idiot's tale.

XIII

Though good writing can be on a modest scale

IF YOU GET "nothing" from the last two chapters "but a gray blur" you will not conclude that you are not a writer. A reader who found nothing in the original draft to set her teeth in creates as she goes along in just the way those chapters were intended to suggest. Maybe you do, too. If so, my bets are most of all on you.

Maybe you have felt so often that "it depends" that you do not stop to think about relativity. You may have worked in autumn gardens, following springs and summers, and taken the talk of progress with an inner smile. Caskets going out bump cradles coming in. If you liked an onion or a bunch of grapes it was not for what it led to. And you never expected everything would "get somewhere." You did not wait for physicists to announce a "law of indeterminacy"; you had always understood that weather was not the only thing of which "you just can't tell." You may have always known that the most stable things in a flood is a man or woman who can ride it.

If this is the kind you are, you don't need philosophers. You will naturally keep an eye for things that interest you. And when an interest lasts until it is far enough away so that your private shadow doesn't half conceal it or distort it, you can find ways to make readers interested, too.

You will not be afraid to make up as much of your story as you need to. And you will make sure that the part you make up rings as true as the recollected part. You will not let us know when you are inventing. It will still be your experience that supplies the elements. They will come from long ago and yesterday, and, though they never went together so before, you will make the whole inevitable. For, beneath your conscious thought, you will be matching all the time with your private pattern of the way things are. Your imagination will be using only what you know. And you will discover that you know a lot that you didn't know you knew.

Going about it that way, and being warmly wise, you will never have to give the answer sometimes given when someones shows that the writer did not mean the thing he had implied: "Oh well, it was just a mood." However it may be for some Irish and some women, the results of your earlier emotions will get stirred up by, and slowly stirred in with, your powerful moods.

You will care enough about the thing you write of to be more faithful to the way it really is, to you, than most busy people take the time to be. You will give the object of your interest a new chance. From the way you write readers can be sure you have no salesman's stake or lawyer's fee. And when your interest is partly dislike, disgust, or re-

membered pain they will know you aren't making things
out more muddled and futile than they are as a justifica-
tion for yourself.

I wonder if you would agree that Thomas Wolfe—
though he wrote so fascinatingly that, dipping into the
middle of a novel for half an hour, one stayed and read to
the last page, and then from the beginning—died too soon
to pull himself together and so exaggerated the chaos that
he found in life.

But no. You would not either nod or shake your head at
such a bear trap of a sentence.

You probably do not think about being a great writer,
and you may be annoyed or smile at this little book's
frequent references to the "great" or the "very good." You
are wise not to be too much concerned about your magnitude. But you don't need to be told that there is something fishy about answers that smart young writers often
give when their writing is compared to the best. Except
to someone who was being ridiculously pretentious, you
would hardly say that you were being "merely" entertaining, that you were certainly not trying to teach. If you did
you know that you would be pulling someone's leg. And to
yourself, at any rate, you would never defend your writing
as the sort of thing "they" seem to like, and editors are
buying. You have pleasures and amusements that go too
deep.

And you are learning, every day, how to play when you
really care. You don't need gravity abolished while you
kick up your heels. With you it isn't either being serious
or having fun. You can be amused with Shakespeare over
things that make you sad. And you would not resent his
double play on "dust" in his lovely song from *Cymbeline*:

> Golden lads and girls all must
> Like chimney sweepers come to dust.

If being philosophical is for those who cannot go ahead until they try to figure everything all out, you understand that make-believe is for those who dare not care.

XIV

And your point of view is
no one's business

NEITHER YOU nor I nor anyone should take your point of view in hand. Don't even worry about having one. Just fend all supervision off, and keep on doing, looking, following attractive whiffs that come to your own nose. "Who acts," according to Aeschylus, "undertakes to suffer," and, if he is right, you will have to take the suffering, too.

First thing you know, someone will be saying, "You don't have the right point of view." And if you go to English classes or listen to talk of literature you will hear a lot about the writer's philosophy of life, and expositions of the scientific, the humanistic, and the neo-Thomist points of view. When connections are made with your own experience and your desires you will be interested. But, still, don't worry about your own.

Remember that seedlings and small live things are healthier without much handling. Notice that when folks talk of the "right" point of view they usually imply one favorable to their own schemes and comfort. You can hardly fail to notice that the writers who most delight and challenge you do not look at anything from quite the angle that any of the broad terms designate. Steele's and

Meredith's divergings from the Augustan and the Victorian points of view will interest you more than their coincidings, if you come to care enough to know the writers as well as your professors know the writers' periods.

You may find that a strong writer's coinciding is more with people, everywhere and any time, than with the special formulations made for periods or special schools. They will probably seem to look with the eyes of human beings and of English, French, or Greeks more than through the lens of any ism. When you like some writer sufficiently to all but jump into his skin you will know that, though he belongs to mankind and to his country, the point of view from which he looks is his alone.

And then you will begin to realize—then or when with some wise and winsome man or woman whom you watch and listen to, as he goes about affairs that he is master of—that a person's point of view is where he looks from. Yours will not be a system you accept. It will not be views that you adopt. If you should tell the world that you are a republican, a Presbyterian, and an abstractionist, some of us might be repelled; none of us would know where you were looking from.

No one appropriates, assents to, or decides upon his point of view. If you should make the attempt, it would be *from* your point of view that you attempted it.

I said "all but jump into his skin" a while ago. Kids used to make it sound like a taunt when they asked, "Where do you live?" And the cocky comeback was, "In my skin! When I jump out, you can jump in." Well, that's no more impossible to do than to know completely another person's point of view. It is the point in the large composition of reality that the individual's private composition has brought him to. It is his inevitable position and his interior attitude. It is the resultant of heredity, the impact of environment on his desires and his susceptibilities, and

the character developed in his responses. It is modified
by every intense emotion, affected by every choice and
every resolution. And the changes in environment, produced either by his reaction to it—as in setting out a tree
or tearing down a shed—or by his moving to a different
town, in turn affect his point of view.

A man's point of view is partly accidental, partly the
consequence of countless choices. It is larger than consciousness, more influential than conscious will. It often
undoes, mocks at, or mends their work. It is at best both
intricate and simple. And when the writer keeps it in-
violate and never tinkers with it, his seeing and his composing from his point of view are authentic. If we never
monkeyed with our point of view it would be as valid as
an orange or a cedar on a mountain. We should "speak"
and write "as one having authority, and not as the scribes."
But that soundness requires the deepest faith, the most
heroic discipline.

When you tell a story or write a poem it is from your
point of view that you select, reject, arrange, make form.
The thing you write about must interest you wholly, must
seem so vital that you accept no current or approved view
of any item of it, but look at every constituent from your
point of view. Then, the way you put details and all together will have form.

The form, if it is akin enough to the reader's, will give
him, as nearly as the limits on human touch permit, the
double blessing of a clear, fresh look at life and a momentary lift from loneliness.

XV

Your style is your surprise

You use all your might to manipulate the memories and proclivities of readers by sleight of word or phrase. But you manipulate your style only as you do your smile. Or do you stand in front of your mirror and practice registering emotions and then, when you are glad or angry, stretch your mouth, tilt your head, and widen or squint your eyes by rote? One who did that would be artificial enough to make up his style.

For style, as Robert Frost says, is the way a man takes himself. And, if you take yourself with so much reluctance that you must always make repairs, your unfavorable opinion is legitimately exposed. Fake style or no style, you give away your secret. Fake style shows you'd rather be thought different from what you are. No style shows that you were willing to give up living in order to exist another dreary day. You may be wanting most to pass a course or to get a good grade from a professor. A few years later you may want a quick, large reputation. You may want several thousand eager mind-improvers to sate their conscientious appetites with figures, facts, and split-second comment in your clever book about the war. Or you may want teachers of all temperaments and many points of view to require of thousands the lugging around of your textbook.

(Some teachers are chronically bored; they have read so many textbooks; or they have read the attempts of students to concoct something invulnerable to the blue pencil. Thanks to those bored teachers and the blue pencil, most themes, honors papers included, lack even the style of a colt or a bull calf, his first day on his feet.)

But once on your own feet, lunging and stumbling, staggering and often tripping, you are on your way to style. As long as you use roller casters you have none. You have lost any style you had begun to show as soon as you mount stilts.

Stilted style, like all fake styles, is a confused acknowledgment of timid admiration. For style we all of us admire. It was half the thrill of Whirlaway. It is the charm of Ingrid Bergman. We quicken to it in Paul Robeson, even if we lack an ear. The world seems good again when cat or country girl or general makes a move with style. We marvel at the confidence, the sureness that we all are looking for. It may be slightly impudent; it may be serene. It is never in two human beings the same.

In even the quiet and modest style of William Dean Howells we can catch twinkles and be surprised by dangerous glints. Religious seventeenth-century Herbert had his reverent and puckish flair. Our Edwin Arlington Robinson, at his best, was funny-sad. Style may be burly-tender as Thomas Hardy's was. It may be flamboyant, teary, gusty, as Charles Dickens's strikes us now. It may be so grimly noncommittal, as Flaubert's was, that it is grim. Style always has a secret that we want.

And if we are caught with style, ourselves, we are surprised. One of the exciting things that come to those who write is having someone say, "I knew it was yours. No one else would think of saying it like that." When that happens to you, you may keep still and not divulge the truth: that you didn't think of saying it any way at all; that your thought was all of what, and not of how. Only you had to say it so that it would work.

Let scoffers mutter "Mystical," the plain fact is that style is a nice surprise. It comes more as gift than acquisition. It is the effectual working of the point of view. It is the grace given by a free imagination. It is of your un-examined depths and all of you. And when all of you is centered—with no part standing off to criticize, admire, or guide—no wonder you show what you did not know you had, and act with style.

The desire to be a writer is not enough. And don't quote Robert Louis Stevenson about the sedulous ape. In the first place, I should reply that the little ape often caught the eraser end of Louis Stevenson's pencil and made his sentence stiff, his story full of unintended creaks. Steven-son was too much the stylist to have style. In the second place, I should reply that Stevenson did not do what he described. He felt the charm, the spell, the bewitchment of the writers and for a while wrote like one and then an-other because his admiration bound him as their thrall.

Writers are compact of paradox, as nature is. And they do their best and damnedest to enthrall. But they are never in possession of themselves and of a style until they are disenchanted from external sorceries. They don't lose pleasure in the best of other writers. But they become pos-sessed by a theme.

If you want to write well, you let a subject make you its subject. It had better, at first, be a small one, big to you with all that it implies. You subject it to yourself. Then you subject one or more readers to it, by the way you master it with words. You make sentences and syllables do what propeller sounds and banking turns of wrist and machine gun noises did for you and all your listeners as you talked of the new P40 when you were in your early teens.

You keep your ear cocked all the time. If you have a subject that possesses you, you will be hard to please. But you do it. You please yourself down to the ground: head, ear, all your senses and desire for balance with firmly planted feet. Then you let the writing cool. You leave it alone for long enough so that, when you read it, you will see not what you felt and thought but what is on the paper. You slash and hew. You snatch things from where they are and put them where they fit. This time, or the fifth time, you get from mere black marks on paper all you meant.

Then you will have written. It may be crude to some maturer person. Don't let that dishearten you. If you are a sophomore you should write as an intelligent sophomore. To sound like Willa Cather or Cardinal Newman when you are only twenty is a shame. Sounding a little callow indicates that your thinking is abreast of your physical and emotional experience, not so far ahead that it will check emotional maturing. Let no one shame you with characteristics natural to your age. You will have more serenity, and excitements will come harder and stir a greater mass as you honestly live more. Poise is enough to start with. Later come the elaborate counterpoises.

Even when you are unmistakably adult, like the late Theodore Dreiser, if your books and stories are lumbering and bumbling, it is ridiculous for you or anyone to try to grace your style. Your style is the way you take yourself. If you take yourself with literal-mindedness and hang-jaw veneration for scientific learning that you were not able to assimilate, but also with ferocious loyalty to sights and feelings you have had, then such will be your style. It is right that the body you were born with, contorted and developed by what you have done, felt, and undergone, should shoulder through your paragraphs. It can't be helped in such a case that your chagrins and fumblings with vain or grotesque love should twist your style or that your envies and resentments, toward people you were reared to treat as betters, should jerk and snarl.

If your style becomes warped and wrung, withered and

acid, there is no use trying to improve it. It is as it must be until you grow. The only way you or anyone who cares for you can help your style is the way of more light and more delight. You might as well tell someone he needs a new self as to tell him to work out a more gracious style. We all do need new selves. We get them only partly, and only as, with luck, we see more and have experiences that melt down our structure and then take shape anew. Joy gives the confidence.

But if we can't just pick a style and have it, Stuart Sherman was right in saying that "Good writing is a matter of natural facility and acquired difficulty." Facile from the first and always means trivial, only of and for the surface, like mud packs.

As your desires take you into the thick of experience, you find yourself bogged down often, up against it many times. No matter how efficient you are, no matter how lucky, you find yourself up the stump, in a hole, or against a wall. You have to stop and look around. You have to take up a notch in your belt, fill your lungs, try the possible way, and, keeping your eyes peeled and your wits about you, move slow and steady with all your might. That happens repeatedly. And when you come to write you take us where you found your meanings. You make the dark places in ourselves accept the light.

From your inner secret all the little quirks and cranks of form derive. And for your reader your pages will be filled with what Ford Madox Ford said were the traits of style, a succession of small surprises. You didn't contrive to put them there. Your style is your surprise.

XVI

And you are original if you just hold your own

NOTHING HURTS a writer more than taking thought to be original. The fear that one will not surprise accounts for a chief ailment of much contemporary poetry. And, curiously enough, it is that fear that makes a lot of it boresomely alike. Unsure of their own force and fire, the poor fellows, who in most things have to take back seats, assume all they can of the tricks and foibles of two or three of the poets most frequently acclaimed. What, of course, they never get is Hart Crane's or Father Hopkin's originality. But they get abundant mannerisms, and they have the joy of puzzling quite as much as the innovators who had complex things to say.

It is much the same in prose. Those who would give anything to write like Saroyan, Proust, or Jimmy Farrell apparently never noticed that their heroes do not write like anyone. The unkindest cut is often inflicted in praise: a new writer is boosted for best-seller as like Steinbeck or Maugham. In the neophyte stage no one can be wondered at or blamed for picking up his hero's way of spitting, growling monosyllables, or scratching. Ten-year-olds carrying bats beside the shortstop of the year. But before originality develops they must start off on their lonely own.

For when self-confidence first rears its head it always seems to keepers of the order very like a pest. It must be isolated, and if possible suppressed. Well, when we are philosophical that state of things seems fair enough.

Inertia, in society and in thought, in patterns of behavior, is what maintains. It is the governor that keeps the energy from wasting, holds it to the operation of the food and comfort machines. Whatever is new yet useful must prove itself against suspicion and the resistance of everything inert. A flicker of confidence is not enough. It must be a steady, not too flapping, flame. Often it survives by being surrounded by cupped hands. It gets going, often, out by the rubbish heap, begins in dumps. The less it is taken seriously for a while, the luckier. For the smart custodians of the status, in literature as in politics and business, take on the slightly cocky fellow, flatter him on his "new ideas," and put him up front to lead—in leading strings.

It takes confirmation of native headstrongness, by success in going it unpleasantly alone, to develop "preternatural self-confidence," the confidence and clear desire that neither man's nor nature's pressures can divert. So, let's not be too sorry that the original have hard going for a while. Let them endure toughness, while the stoutness of their fibers and the flavor of their sap become incorrigible. They have to be rugged in ways not dreamed of by gunmen or marines. It is a strain for nature to produce gentleness and sweetness that will keep. Fineness does not readily develop the resilience, and the capacity to take an edge, of tempered steel.

How does it ever happen? How do a few retain and solidify the uniqueness that lies in nearly every baby basket? The facile answer is that the power to originate comes by a freak of nature. Many of us take consolation in supposing that to produce something authentically new is to be a freak. When the doer is dead or widely recognized we shelve him—and the question—in a safely lofty niche, embarrass his head with wreaths and halos, inscribing "genius" at his cemented feet.

But the one exceptional trait that original people really

have in common is the energy to reject the warnings that parents and companions, the weather and sticks and stones conspire to enforce. Told, more times than the meek among us, "You can't have your own way; not in this man's world," they flashed their eyes and squared their jaws and walked away, and little by little they *had* it. They had it and they made it. And their own way was their style, their message, their meaning.

Yet the original are, also, often so gentle, so unforcing, so willing to move from the worn path, that they seem the meekest of us all. Remember shy Emily Dickinson, for one, Oliver Goldsmith for the absurd variant, and Chaucer, who stared upon the ground as if he were looking for a hair. It isn't bullheadedness.

In his wildness the genuine artist is as much akin to the hermit thrush as to the bear. But he doesn't always move off further into the dark woods. He meets the issue, when it is his, and he stands fast.

The thing of it is, he is not often after what the rest are after; he is still wanting what they once too vaguely wanted and gave up for substitutes. His wildness shows most in the indissuadableness of his desire. He bets his life on what most of us sigh over and, with an unconfessed relief, kiss good-by. He wants a few things, his way; if he can't find them he will make them.

There is no use trying to deny that conventional compromisers would always see something Satanic, not approved in any boss-fearing school, something too diabolic to be dismissed as raising the devil in an original man. "You want too much," we tell him. And we still wonder how he got that way.

One thing that counts for keeping up the original fight is joy. A little rapture, not the guck that goes by that name in Tin Pan Alley songs, but real, top-to-toe, through-and-through delight, once tasted, will take a man through all the disillusionments. Determinism cannot daunt the determination of a man who has been through the valley where hoping is abandoned if he has also known delight. Such a man often sets his heart upon delight for the rest of us.

Take what it may, all you who read this could be, in your own way and degree, original, if you learned to circumvent or sidestep all attempts to shape you, if you kept from being embroiled with those who have the sort of power you claim not to want, if you turned from everything that would compromise your desire, and, giving in wherever your intention was not at stake, you held your own.

XVII

You will hate to be fooled
even by yourself

GOLDEN HAZES and cheap ecstasies are poison ivy and Job's itch to one who has known delight. Like Job, a writer reinforced with that·essential knowledge would rather put up with all the fiend's inventions than be comforted with lies. Not for him a little honey and a little perfume in the caldron of the bearded witch; when he gets his horror portion let the brew be slab and thick.

He will not play fast and loose with his emotions. He declines to call a ripple a tidal wave. Nor will he, like the high diver in the story, plunge into a moist rag. Feelings he has had and the exactingness of his desires supply calipers and plummet. And relativity, itself, marks degrees.

For the lucky, it permits a private measure, also, for sensations. Enough of them are delightful to sharpen and maintain a clear perceptiveness. And crackers and milk do not evoke superlatives if you have properly enjoyed wild duck. It may be well enough, at times, to count your blessings; but every experience with juice and flavor will "teach you differences."

Knowing differences, you can be sure of likenesses. And differences and likenesses are the imagination's wherewithal. The writer is the last person to afford, in anything, to be vague. Not blurring is the more important because his enthusiasms and discriminations soon take him where shapes keep changing, where science, with its exactness and its necessary controls, finds nothing measurable to report.

Veils, draperies, perfume, and veneer, the writer does not lose the childhood impulse to lift, part, sniff close to, and pry off. He may accept some; first he must make sure what is behind, beneath. Illusions interest him; he knows they are produced by something real. He does not scorn an onion. Tears, taste, and nourishment are quite as undeniable as is the fact that when you peel off all the curving tissues you have nothing in your grasp. The secret is the composition. And if you are going to be a writer you are not sad but glad to know.

You would not be one who thinks that ducks go around with sage and bread crumbs, raisins and chestnuts, beaten eggs, salt, and celery in their insides. You would rather get your fingers soiled and bloody as, with sucking sound, you draw out windpipe, lights, and guts. The good texture, smell, and stomach satisfaction of breast meat, liver, and stumpy leg, particularly if the duck is wild, are your as-

surance that plain fact has no rival in flattered ignorance
or make-believe.

The juice that flows when teeth clamp down in venison
lubricates disdain of plaster of Paris meat and *papier
mâché* fruit. And the more fleshly succulence and winter-
green and cinnamon your vigorous appetites rustle and
wrangle from your world, the more spiritual intolerance
you grow for being gulled and duped. You come to like
buttermilk and the inner bark of cherry twigs. The thing
you cannot stand is sauce that makes all neutral and
alike.

When your own pretenses gag you and you prefer black
widow spiders in your bedroom to the daintiest humbug,
and your *bête noire* is your own blah, then you have the
rudiments of taste. You can forgive and understand
gradual, deliberate confusions and frightened little shams,
that no longer work on you; you avoid them.

For who knows better the way small make-believes
grow wool over eyes and knot together, so that soon what
you just pretended is all that you can see? Some things
have to be momentarily brushed aside. After recognition,
it is waste to reckon and assess your weaknesses and brood
upon your failures. But nothing, even for a moment, has
to be seen or felt as it is not.

No writer achieves complete clarity. But the nearer he
comes to seeing clearly, the more his gifts prevail. Keeping
exposed and having strong desires, you may experience
more frustrations than the common run. They condense
you, give you what boiling gives to maple sap. You achieve
a richer concentrate. Vapidness is driven off.

And the fibers of your being get more sinewy with the
greater use that repeated attempts require. The grit that
made the friction gets embedded in your cells. And thus
you keep and develop your sensitiveness while you grow
more tough. Your shell is not between you and more

experience; instead you have corundum through and through.

A boy playing with a horseshoe crab, that first doubled his shell and pointed his barbed tail over his curved front and then flattened out and showed the slightness of his vital part, remarked, "This bird is mostly shell, and he's not got much to hide behind it." Protective insensitiveness and delusion are for those who never felt the big elations, for those who never cared enough for joy to incur pain.

XVIII

Caring that much, you can't miss contradictions

It isn't optimistic naïveté that keeps you trying to create. The intensity of delight that helps to a clear mind also leaves you acutely susceptible to ironies commonly glossed over. Declining to be satisfied with the gaudy panels in the circus parade, you are bothered when you gaze through the iron bars: a tiger being fed a butcher's cut. You shake your head and grin at the suggestion that he be left unfed and loose to feed on you. And yet—

You feel uncomfortable without a thing to say, waiting around with others to see the crashed airplane engine dragged ashore; when you read advice, opposite the editorials, to conquer shyness by forcing yourself to say something, interestingly and in a commanding voice, you, nevertheless, fling the paper down.

You find that in the perfect winter climate, along with flowers and all the birds, are smudge pots against the frost, morning fogs that make breakfast napkins clammy, and many rains. You learn of three kinds of deadly snakes, scorpions, and wild cats where you would like to look for birds, sharks and sting rays where you swim, cockroaches and mosquitoes inside cottages.

Unless screened against experience by servants, you can't ignore the greasy dishpan following roast lamb, the dirty diapers of the cutest baby, or gray rings inside the bathtub of the most stimulating lecturer of the year.

Ironies do not die down, for you who care, as you grow up, or even old. Say you are old enough to have a son, and he is bending poor nails, trying to fasten an unused fence picket of the hardest wood where it will give more elevation to an antenna; so you go to help him, find the stoutest nails, and, with some difficulty and some vanity, affix the picket. Meanwhile your son has gone off with an angry fling. And when you go back into the house he insists, his face taut with held-back tears and fury, that what you did is wrong. As he goes out and jerks down your work and patiently, with careful thought and skill, this time carries out his plan, you reflect that if you want him to be independent and sure of his desires, if you want him resolute in making possibilities, seen in day-dreams, into facts, you cannot shame him for his fierce refusal of your help.

If you take a job with the government you soon discover that either you must give up, to keep your wishes for a better spread of human well-being pure, or else you must risk not only opposition and defeats but a plunge to the melee that will frazzle and stain the garments of your innocence. Not that you will sell out. But, to get something done, you will struggle and rush, fend off, and make allies, and, first thing you know, will no longer have clean hands. It will only have been worth while, as it was with Lincoln and with Franklin Roosevelt, if the setup for us all becomes a little fairer. The only way to keep immaculate is not to act.

As a young officer in the army you may have had troubled moments, realizing that, in giving yourself to fend off statehood from selfhood, you had to be personally involved in setting organization above the persons in it. You mitigated the brutality a trifle, here and there, but you could not keep free of it. And if you could have you would not have been sitting back to benefit by others' violence. None of us alive escaped that contradiction in the war.

And, peace or war, we all of us cause suffering and rouse resentment by well-meant acts. Polite acquaintances may keep us for years in ignorance, if we like to be deceived. But we can't act without someone's wishing we would not disturb the peace, someone's being annoyed at our not doing what we do in his way.

Even love, in action, involves commitments that constrain. Some freedom disappears as soon as two desires join. And often the desire at the root of love induces now one and now the other to yield his own desire to go or stay, to get where they were going, or to linger and enjoy. Only often-fired, remembering affection, with determination holding and imagination intervening, can prevent a permanent relationship from becoming too much constraint.

In every pot of ointment soon appears a fly. Your good fortune lies in not needing to forget it or deny it. In every situation hides some creative chance.

XIX

You cannot ignore conflicts
that will not subside

MUCH that is ironical in civilization, much that causes misery occurs because we try to get effects without waiting for the motives. Angry and contemptuous, we try to get the effect of loving our neighbor and beam at him with syrup in our voice. How many children must have thought, "If she would only call me dirty skunk instead of dear!" Frequently it seems politeness is to do and say the meanest thing the kindest way. Everybody knows the disgust that goes with saying thank you for a generous-seeming act when the warm and kindly feeling that impels such acts, at best, is just not there.

Usually we love a person who is feeling on top of the world, friends with all he meets and overflowing with fun and joy of life; the more such a person makes our own step light, the more we are nauseated at the feigned high spirits of the breakfast-food announcer and the deep-voiced paeans for laxatives.

But, admiring generous and gracious people, envying those who have real charm, can we continue unaffected and be brusque and awkward till our natures change? Few dare to wait until they have the feeling, the impulse in their vitals.

Those few whose acts are generally determined by un-sophisticated motives may delight us and win our deepest trust; they also disappoint us, badly, and often anger us.

It is when thus hurt or vexed that we get moral. We

quote Paul on charity. We argue against their inconsistency. And we fall into the trap of implying that we want them to be warm, or tolerant, or cheerful, not because they feel that way, but because it is "right."

"Let people be natural," some one says, "and if they're tired or bored or grieved, let them act that way." "Oh," the comeback is, "you want everybody to act natural but me. I feel like complaining of their nasty moods."

There we have a sample of a conflict in which every writer is forced to engage. And it isn't as simple as Rousseau or the late Professor Babbitt, Paul of the New Testament or D. H. Lawrence makes it seem. Who can live in a city, work in an office, or go to school, to say nothing of being a member of a family, and act only in accordance with the way he feels? If one does so, he forces others more than ever to conceal, suppress, disguise.

The decision of society, in every century and generation, seems to be that it is better to act *as if* you had the feelings that the people around you like. Knowing the weakness of the flesh, the so-called "mature" usually take that program as the straight line, and tolerate waverings and weavings. If moral pressure is not sufficient, we put on brass knuckles, and compel men to stay along that line. Thus such peace and order as we have, with insanity, crime waves, and wars to take off the surplus pressure, has been evolved.

To most poets and men of imagination that social sham is not fit to bow before. The balanced, worldly, and winkingly serene, like Horace, may accept it. Even they expose and mock at calculated pieties and cold proprieties.

But what would you do? Sharp senses, strong desires, sensitiveness to qualities, and the consequent imagination will force you into such dilemmas by the score.

One more sample: perhaps you enjoy George Gershwin's "I got plenty of nuttin." Perhaps you feel that what

Porgy had and exulted in is also enough for you. And then you find yourself with just about as few possessions; you have your gal, and she is going to have a baby, and you are rather scared. You want her to have the very best of care and aid. And you wish you had provided.

How about it? Where will you take your stand? There is another conflict for you. If you are going to have anything as good as Du Bose Heyward had to say about it, you will have to make up your own mind. Not once for all. But in many small decisions you may find something even better than that good song.

You will find your own major conflicts. And most of them will not seem major at the time. They will be small, immediate issues, and you may determine some of them offhand. Others will not stay settled. And you will be tantalized and sometimes driven almost frantic. But people will be counting on you; in some predicaments your fate will be obviously at stake. You can't let them slide. You can't merely take heads or tails of a flipped coin.

Let us keep this chapter short. You find the illustrations for the following sample dilemmas. You will, soon or late. My present attitude on some of them has already been implied. But being a different person you cannot permanently appropriate mine. You can't even appropriate Bergson's or Kant's, Dante's or those of Jesus Christ.

Which comes first, the individual or society?

How much freedom should we give up for equality?

Is kindness more needed than independent men and women?

Which is more precious, a sure dependence or adventure?

Shall we shut off grossness and by the same barriers keep out greatness?

Should skepticism be allowed to menace faith?

Should faith be allowed to limit intelligence?

Which shall you seek first, clarity or a realization of all the shades, variations, and ins-and-outs?

Is devotion to people, *à la* Voltaire, more important or devotion to God, *à la* Pascal?

Which are you, animal or "a god, though in the germ"?

XX

And of which you often cannot take one side

G. K. CHESTERTON, the late life-loving essayist, is a good writer by whom to be introduced to paradox. Not that he is the greatest revealer of paradoxes among writers in our century; he had such fun with paradoxes that he used them too lavishly. But he is not easy for a person who has wrestled long with conflicts to dismiss. You could do worse than read his *Heretics* or *The Victorian Compromise*. A subtler and greater master is J. M. Synge. William Blake, sometimes fantastic, often shows us truth by turning a truism upside down. Montaigne is great. Plato's Socrates will do. Shakespeare is the greatest I have found.

Sometimes Chesterton oversimplifies the conflict and lustily proclaims the unfashionable side. In doing so he was relatively honest; he not merely wrote but acted by his choice. But Synge, and the great ones, often find it impossible to choose. That sounds like inability to make up their minds. But right there is the catch. It is the clue to catch for greatness—if you have enormous energy and a passionate realization of both pulls.

This is the catch: in not choosing, the great ones make

instead of a selection a reconcilement. Now a reconcilement looks, both to zealous choosers and to mugwumps anxious for corroboration of their fear to choose, the same as compromise. But it is the antithesis: a composition of the vitals of the opposites.

Life approaches you, so to say, with both hands behind her back, and says, now with a smile and now with a frown, "Which hand will you take?" You are man enough or woman enough to have learned the folly of not making up your mind. You watch for a twitching sleeve, a betraying glance, you look to see if one shoulder is a trifle low, you lunge and try to peek. And finally you choose. Perhaps your sufferings or your pities make you presume the truth is on her left. Perhaps your desire to conserve the gratifications you are sure of or the moral association of the word makes you take the right.

But suppose you have indelible memories of delight, and have been through the slough of despond, clear through and reached the further bank. Then you may take, even with Life, the initiative. You play, but not the game of either-or. You have that "preternatural" confidence and the love for fatal gambles that goes with it. With a prayer to the creative intention, that you believe potentially superior to clockwise life, you give a long transfixing look and suddenly snatch both gifts, from right and left.

Perhaps they are incompatible as fox and goose, as being a good neighbor and standing for your rights, or as being faithful to the highest possibility you have discovered in your daydreams and making a decent living for all your family. It will test all the faith generated by your joys, the force developed in your fights; you will need the patience to induce harmless dove and wily serpent to co-operate.

This is all a metaphor. If many read it, some will sneer and sniff. All I reply is: I have seen it done. All the really great have done it. Not perfectly. Not utterly. Relatively, and well enough to prove that human beings can be better and wiser than most of us are. They prove that joy, irony, tragedy, and faith can coexist.

XXI

You back both sides till violent encounter becomes engendering embrace

You UNDERSTAND that nobody goes systematically about this fusing of opposites. You cannot arrange it. But if you have witnessed creative outcomes you may be less afraid when the violence begins in you. It happens because a person who has known renunciation has also known intensely the satisfactions of experience on both sides. His great reluctance to give up what he cares about prevents either side from showing the white flag.

I knew a robust and skillful writer who, twice, in plain ways gave the verdict to one side. He had a curious, avid mind and he wanted influence. He wanted a position in which he would be listened to. He went to graduate school. There he hated much of the mechanism and the antipersonal procedure. Inwardly he writhed at the grim seriousness about secondary matters and the frivolous ignoring of primary ones. But he took one horn of his dilemma, silenced his disgust, and stayed.

His other plain case of drastic choosing concerned natural differences with his parental family. He went through the weaning process common to the vigorously intelligent. But he did not resolve the conflict in a still fruitful and affectionate relationship; he severed all relations with those nearest to his blood, because they were not near his thought.

He took his degree with distinction and became a famous professor before he was thirty. And for years he was known to serious readers as a feared and reverenced anti. Suddenly he renounced teaching, became a leading literary journalist, and, to the amazement of admirers, a still more redoubtable pro—praising the very writers and philosophic accents that he had denounced. On both sides he was not only brilliant but honest; on both, though deserving admiration, he was something less than great. Now his once constantly seen name is seldom mentioned. He has died in circumstances implying that his heart, literally and perhaps figuratively, was weary of this world. The measure of his influence is slighter than he hoped.

I know another writer about the first one's age. He also has always been curious and had an active mind. He went to college at the university where the first one took his Ph.D. For about two years he studied with distinguished teachers and took delight in Latin and some of the philosophy. But he soon felt that neat academic oversimplifications were not for him, and quietly disappeared. He could not stay against his feelings; he would not abandon education. He continued learning, did much uncertificated teaching, and later was called back to the same seat of culture, for years to fill to overflowing the public lecture auditorium and to teach.

He, too, had disagreements with his family; he, too, went his separate way in thought and act. But he managed to preserve a warm relation with his next of kin. And now, as he grows older, having, in spite of external maiming and distress, always had the buoyance to get up above clashing opposites where he could see to put them together, he is serene. And, slowly, without interfering, he is showing many Americans how to imagine and grow wise.

Both these men had extraordinary gifts and bold intentions. One domesticated his dilemmas and made pets of them until he could round up and drive most of the wild herd, mounted on one that he had taken by both the horns. The other stoutly took one horn in many a brave encounter, till at the end his heart was gored.

Two very young men could be similarly contrasted from intimate acquaintance. One I watched make specific surrendering choices. The other achieved some quiet, gradual resolutions. The chooser has long since written a bestseller; the slow resolver is an unknown man just out of uniform, getting ready to be a writer about, and for, more than the clocked day.

You begin to realize the difference: between simplifying conflicts and enduring violent tussles of opposed desire within yourself till the heat of conflict rises to the heat of pairing, and clash changes to a clasp.

XXII

Resulting humor whisks you through the wall behind the clock

HUMOR attends the embraces of incompatibles. Who knows whether it is the condition of their occurring or their consequence? Certain it is that we gain composure in the presence of irony by having many former ironies composed within us. And equally certain is it that the less

sense we have of humor the more we have to simplify,
evade some facts, make up our minds too soon.

Humor mischievously furnishes time out. When your
feelings and other people's feelings are about to catapult
you into something futile and foolish, you suddenly think
of always, alongside of now, and pause. And the pause is
just enough for a new and oblique start. You regain your
balance in that timeless flash of clearness.

Humor frisks the minute to make incompatibles unite.
(We earnest people—whom atom bombs and dated obliga-
tions to salvage civilization keep on the jump and on the
dot—miss that "waste of time.")

No matter how you say it, humor always sounds a little
underworldly. It is of the demimonde, not more than half
of this world. It may take you into the sort of rapscallion
company that Villon frequented. You are tarred in some
part of your anatomy with the same brush as Falstaff. And
I guess you have to face it: humor is not saintly.

But don't accept the word of humorous people that they
are not heroic. It is true that they are seldom brought home
upon their shields; they live to fight another day. But
laughing off responsibility is not humor. Humor comes
out of conflicts, not from avoiding them. To be sure, it is
the horse worth a kingdom that whirls you off to where
you can know before you choose, can reconcile instead of
choose. It picks its own occasions, seldom the "appropriate
and fit." You have heard on many occasions—it happens
chiefly on "occasions"—the vain attempts to trot it out. Try
to harness humor and all you have is the dangling harness
to trip over and wave around.

Humor is always touch and go. It helps you to a kind
of freedom because it is never anything but free. It sometimes whisks you right through into the flux where blank
walls yield, endless circles are but spiral eddies, and things
hard and fast become susceptible of new composition.

When you swing back into time your puniness is funny more than awful; the terrible crisis, dwindling, leaves room for composing possibility with fact.

Swinging back and forth between the patterned world of clock and calendar and the darkling flux, you keep out of bondage: to others, your own past and future, even God.

At moments when you have present to your mind both the systematic, static order of *as if,* that we call real, and the shift and continual new forming of earth, water, stars, and wind, and are given, therefore, the daring to bring together opposites, you can talk with those whose timid trust is almost all in seeming. You are not too concerned if for a while they miss your ominous-encouraging overtones. And maybe some of them, hardly noticing and unalarmed, will begin to feel for themselves the mocking hope. If so, humor has whisked your audience and they know once more the serenity of fear that is also faith, though clock-ticks and machines that run on schedule had them all but hypnotized.

Beguiled by you they begin to see that schemes and plans blow away like mists along the road, and foundations set to stand forever against the flood always wash away. Then they are free to see that dreamed-of possibilities gain worth by being set up in the world of time; and creation is always to be done. Seeing that they can live only on a double scale, they can smile and relax. As participants in work that's never done, they can laugh at everything that's fixed and rigid. If anything saves the world from fission and chain reactions it will be the counterexplosion of many chuckles.

XXIII

And from out the play of persistent opposites also emerge your stories

CONFLICT and creation go on forever. Hence the stories, the tragedies, and the fun.

No matter what a woman does to a man he never becomes quite a woman. Both men and women are always doing what they can to reform their opposites. Sons and husbands are often comic products. So are wives and daughters. But in every generation the liveliest, most fruitful matches seem to result from incorrigible masculinity, maleness, manly frailty and incompleteness, in the man, and femininity, femaleness, and womanly incompleteness in the woman. They never quite reach the harmony talked of when they got engaged; they never quite fight it to a finish. They just fight and love until the light goes out.

Men do, however, make some women reasonable. They give them degrees and subordinate positions. But they seldom marry them. And if they do they seem to lose their interest. We like to find that our dominations do not last. We are glad the land cannot fill up the sea, the sea wash down the land.

And as the artist comes closer and closer to encompassing and composing instead of taking sides, he becomes more able to show, instead of arguing or being didactic. He need not champion knives and run down forks or spoons. He shows them interacting, with now and then a comical ascendancy, now and then an effective but wavering co-operation. Sometimes the knife neatly pushing potato against the back of the fork's tines, sometimes the fork managing the vegetables alone. Here a knife will take too much upon him. There he will be kept in waiting till the going is really tough. Spoons often, for a while, have things all their way. But the author, showing us, remembers that predominance like that does not last. He makes us realize that each of us, as knife, fork, or spoon, is an element of a composition, and that if we want to be a determinant we have to be components. He charms and dares us to be responsible and take our chances. He helps us to see chances and gives encouragement by taking his. Playfully he discloses that the set of which knife, fork, or spoon is one component is what it has become not only because of the heavy handle and sharp edge of the knife, the multiple pointedness of the fork, or the containing capacity of the spoon, but by interplay.

And the critic or the teacher who has loved the free play of such authors in the act of determining form, will not tell how to write short stories. He knows

> There are nine and ninety ways of constructing tribal lays
> And — every — single — one — of — them — is — right!

Not so very many stories are good enough, to be sure, to set right the mathematics professor and chairman of the library committee who congratulated his college on the lessening proportion of mere fiction in the students' reading. Of all the millions only a few hundred are great stories. Those few are better worth a growing human being's time than whole libraries of speculation and statistics. Of those great ones the formula is good only for the individual story.

Therefore a teacher can only show. He can show this twist and that trick in a particular story he admires. He can read a young writer's story aloud so that the whole class recognizes the admirable aliveness of one of the characters, as the story opens, and the way his inner state becomes plain, so that we experience his feelings, because of what he does and says. In another story he can show the cowardice of the writer's point of view, exposed in the too luscious rhetoric. In another he can show the implication emerging, as a piece of dialogue unfolds. He can show the use of characteristic turns of speech, at once forwarding the action and delineating the configuration of a person. Reading, that way, with those who want to write, he can spread before them myriads of possibilities, a few of which each learning writer may some day find possible for him.

He can show most by sympathetically and co-operatively imaging the story that the novice tries to write, then asking questions, touching mainly on the substance, and on this word, that scene, the shaping of a certain paragraph.

Last and least he can throw out suggestions, to be taken with plenty of salt, through the filter of previous experience. And only the suggestions apart from the palpitating tissues of attempted stories can be given in this book.

The other slight delinquency of how-to-write-short-story books, except Ring Lardner's skit, is this: analysis gives you components; the one thing it cannot give is the composition. And composition happens to be the one thing needful, the only thing that counts. It is the one thing that every time is new.

So, now, having first sealed my lips and then tied my tongue, I will suggest.

Once at Yaddo, a man who had published stuff of mine and then expressed a wonder what was so good about it after all was mentioned in the grandiose dining room as a strange former guest. I asked Evelyn Scott, who was as lovely as her novels were strong, what she thought of him. My voice indicated the tone of answer I expected. In the way of the abler of the fluent writers one met at Yaddo,

Evelyn Scott paused to think. Like a young girl in the Virgil class confessing that she had translated only up *to* that line, she said, "I am afraid I cannot give him as I see him, in anything I say." She smiled in deprecation. "I think I could make you see him in a story."

What she distrusted was not her own insight, of course; it was the truth of any intellectual short cut to comprehending a crossed and faltering soul. She would keep still or write a story. In a story she could so show him that the reader would *see* why he did what he did, how he had become what he was. And there would be compassion more than scorn.

To make us see is the responsibility the storyteller assumes. In *Story* several years ago appeared a disappointing story by an amusing Irishman who had once been in a freshman class of mine. It presented but did not show. The writer observed, was moved, but withheld his answer, and got out of answering by being very neat, concise, and truthful about details.

The excuse of leaving the reader freedom was no good. You cannot ask the reader what he makes of something until you know what to make of it. Artistic reticence is not evasion. The writer need not let out any wisp of interpretation. The good one indicates how he takes the characters and the action. The composition shows.

XXIV

A good story is an experience

IF YOU LIKE PEOPLE enough to puzzle over them and to be discontented with attempts to put them in a nutshell you may show us things it pleases you to figure out, in stories. How you tell the stories also has to be a matter of trial and error, of fortunate figuring out.

Sometimes it proves good to have begun at some clearly marked beginning and moved chronologically. Sometimes the story seems to move straight forward and yet the reader finds he is continually discovering more and more about what the characters did before the story opened. Sometimes the movement is like a shuttle, crosswise, but always a little further on. Sometimes time order is reversed. And sometimes we see the characters at landing fields of a long flight: the action alights three or four times; each time there is a happening and a look back to understand, and in the following paragraph the action lets us come close again, 'way on beyond. And one much-used natural method is to begin in the middle of things, move back a little, then forward, all the time traversing both a circumference around the entire situation and an axis line from pole to pole. There can be no table of determinants, like directions about when an amateur fisherman should use this fly or that. You have to trust a hunch and try.

It is the same with scenes. In a short story there obviously cannot be many. But, one or three, and mostly scene or mostly straight narration with one climactic scene, there are no rules. It is good to be acquainted with many permutations and combinations of technique; but no system for selecting and combining deserves your trust.

Affectionate and admiring study of many good stories makes one feel that, in story-writing, going by guess and by God is not inexpert but the inevitable creative way. How much conversation should you employ? The answer is, God knows; it is up to you to gamble on your impulse and find out. The same with determining the point of view from which you will have your reader watch. Usually I prefer one point of view throughout, and usually the point of view of one of the two or three principal characters. But I enjoyed a story by Pearl Buck the other day in which the reader was put successively inside about five different men and women in the story. It was not confusing; it did not, that time, diminish the dramatic play.

You, as one story writer, may come to be positive and dogmatic on such a question as whether the first person should or should not be used, or whether a planted narrator, like Conrad's Marlow, is right. It is inevitable that vigorous natures that have worked out important decisions should feel that they are binding. They are, fortunately, for the individual writer. Another good writer may legitimately be equally certain about an opposite choice. A third may use both ways and still others, and smile at certainty.

A few things we can all be sure of: that explanations should follow, not precede, aroused interest; that, as much as possible, it is good for the reader to get story while he is also getting needful exposition; that every speech and every motion should do at least three things—advance the action, reveal character, and disclose some clutch or push or slip in a dynamic relationship; that the first and last are Alpha and Omega—the opening and the closing, of story, scene, section (supposing you have sections), paragraph and sentence are places of great attention from the reader, and should be taken advantage of, with skill, and never allowed to seem mechanically used.

And it appears sure to me that every good story is more than a record; that every good story is more than a segment of reality; that every good story is more than a fillip to the nerves; and that every good story is more than an idea. What is common to all good ones is that, in reading and digesting the story, the reader goes through an experience. After a good story and the assimilation of it you are a more experienced person.

I know that sounds a little extravagant. But what a story lacks in factuality, in literal and completed cycles of sensation and response, in chances for you to fix your own attention and make comebacks of your own, is, in varying degrees, made up for by the advantage of the reader's being lent an imagination always more specially focused on certain realities and relations and, usually, more developed and, yes, more energetic than his own. For an extreme corroboration of this belief that good fiction can be a real experience, I recall the assertion of an extraordinarily imaginative man, himself a successful writer, that Proust's *A la recherche du temps perdus* was a more important experience for him than all of his own private experiences combined. Too bad, if true. But to induce experiences is the writer's attempt. An attempt so staggering, as I have said, that it ought to keep him humorous.

To achieve the potency of experience he must make his story both move and extend, in space. Good inferences from a writer's own experience, supported by fit and vivid details, can yet so fail to make a story that the writer may hear a good friend say, "It sounds like a synopsis." (I won't say how I know.)

Time and recurrences of impressions must be allowed or experience will not occur. The story must not be a sip; it must be a kettleful. It must have thickness, substance, a chance for realizations to grow on you. The reader must have the unconscious feeling of breathing the air, looking around, getting the lay of the land, and gradually making out who is who and what is up.

The writer must get the reader to having visceral and motor responses, the way in a car the person beside the driver invisibly puts on the brake. He must get the whole intricate loom of desires and feelings, that compose the story, whizzing, clamping, spreading, and crossing in the reader's body and mind, as colored threads shoot transversely back and forth, spools vibrate on their spindles, and the pattern slowly weaves. And, when the fabric is all tied and cut, he must leave the reader with both an upward impulse and a kind of peace.

XXV

With people

IF YOU WANT to get into the big money as a story writer you do not want people. You want trappings with a dummy inside. The dummy must be very beautiful, very smart, very quaint, very sinister, very masterful, or very mysterious. And it must be so unparticularized that almost any bleached bone or bag of entrails can identify himself. For the unavowed purpose of such fiction, aside from income to the author and time-killing for the reader, is to save us the trouble, when we are in danger of seeing how vain and brief we are, of dreaming our own daydreams.

For the biggest money you must make all the trappings extremely authentic. Be sure your reader keeps feeling both "Boy, this is the life!" and "Gosh, that certainly is the way things are!" Advertisers will make it possible to pay vast sums to writers who can help you fool yourself and at the same time put suspicion out of the question.

And yet that is seldom or never the way the "top" writers for "top" magazines think they write. They aren't catering; they haven't recently sold out. They think the way they write! They have cheated themselves around so many clocks that they have come to think, in all seriousness, that the possession of expensive things is a proof of wisdom. They really think a lady is a person in whose presence one would not acknowledge that venereal disease has to do with the same magic that makes the heroines of their stories lustrous. They really think a gentleman is one who would not read Dos Passos out loud "before the family hearth." And they think a democrat is one who will play poker with someone from the wrong side of the tracks as soon as he owns slums enough to erect a "refined and tasteful" home in a "congenial" suburb.

The smartest of these word-artisans have a corner-drugstore wit and wisdom, bland and pseudo-audacious; they dare mock at those whose small change amasses gradual millions for them. The young and the gray-haired "professional writers," of this main-tent sort that I have known are idealists. They are earnest, they are sweet, they are fertile; and almost everybody likes them and admires the denominations of their checks. But if this book is really about writers, they are not writers at all. At least one of them could teach me things about writing, and he may not have given up forever the real thing. But in spite of borderline writers of great experience and some gifts, this little book makes no provision for writing that puts persuasion above shaping genuine experience; it makes no provision for writing that is sappy-soothing like a crooner's song:

> Kid yourself along, Kid
>   Hum a song,
> You may get a break, Kid,
>   Join the throng.
>
> You don't have to rate, Kid,
>   Trust your fate,
> Miracles will come, Kid —
>   Just you wait.

In terms of this book a writer is a person who creates an illusion for the joy he takes in prowess and secretly for the sake of increasing human mastery in the composition of experience. In other words the writer is still learning how to make meaning. In the waist of his hourglass he is seizing and shaping newly as the sand grains fall. He writes of what he learns.

For a writer who knows life and still risks creation, one sure thing is that a good story must have one or two people in it who are real. And to be real they must be particularized, not quite like anyone else you ever saw, as each real person is. We all know lots of people who fit the description of the Athenians, in the first book of Thucydides' *History of the Peloponnesian War,* that ends, "they are made neither to be quiet themselves, nor let the rest of the world be so"; but we do not know any of them unless we know his typicalness *in relation* to, say, the way he runs his tongue along his upper lip. And the fun comes in, for the story writer, in keeping the story interesting, in providing little expectancies and little surprises all the way, while playing the commonness against the specialness and matching the matter-of-factness of real people. But beware of literal-minded fidelity to the actual person who gave you the nucleus of your character. If you are too strong-willed in your loyalty, the character will die and stink. It's when the character goes and interferes with your plan that you know he is alive. He probably will not be the person that you started with, after another lively person in the story has flung a quip or a defiance. Each person and each act must be partly product and partly cause, and everything in play.

With all the pulling and hauling, the affection and resistance, and each one's being what the others condition him to be and, at the same time, being a force and an uncertainty, there will be plenty of unshed tears and soundless laughs, much tension and many changes in the tension. You will not add or much arrange; you will insist only that, all the time, the motion and the tension shall be to you *as if* you were witnessing an actual situation.

You can know your characters as you know no one, actually, in real life. You may come near to knowing yourself, at times, and you need to in order to be able to write stories at all. But your characters you can realize as pathetic even at the moment when they—like you in real life at such moments—feel that they are grand. You know they are strong when they are feeling scared and almost beaten. And you know they are funny when they are most certain that they know the score. You know all the intricate web of motives in them, and that a little extra pull on one thread will make the behavior altogether different from what it would have been with a slight pull, instead, on another thread. It is hard to make sure constantly that nothing happens, in your people and their relations, that you would not bet your neck would happen the same way in actual life.

When you read short stories by Chekhov you probably never doubt the authenticity. It seems as actual as the yawns and the rustling pages of magazines, the smart and decrepit luggage, the cheery chatter of the chief clerk and assistants, and the variety of farewells and welcomes in a long wait at a January bus station. But, for a while, perhaps you wonder why Chekhov wrote the story, how he expected anyone to be interested. Soon you begin to be more clear about the feeling that it gave you, and you know that, for once, a writer has given you realizations, with materials of your own experience, that you could not have had without his aid.

For Chekhov is a master at the most exacting kind of imagination: inventing things as mixed and ordinary and mainly low in relief as the greater part of real life, and giving them such a rhythm and tension that, without the usual "heightening," they mean more to the reader than the same things would have meant if they had happened before his eyes. The unemotional Chekhov felt everything with sympathy. He endows with significance the manner of lifting off a kettle or the changed inflection of a growl.

If you are imaginative all the time you won't have to heighten when you write. But be sure that at least one character is interesting to the point of genuine excitement, for you. He must be unique and a recognizable force, a person, though in real life college students might dismiss him as "that bum."

XXVI

In which someone turns a corner
or a hair

KATHERINE ANNE PORTER, a gallant rider of dilemmas, retold Chekhov's story about the man who didn't die, in a *Saturday Evening Post* contest for retellings of favorite stories. The contest editor sent it back: "No plot, my dear, no story."

Which end is up? The "top" (-pay) magazine turns down the top story of the top master of the short story retold by one of the top contemporary prose writers? Well, writers are used to a topsy-turvy world. They can take the surprise of each specific case of relativity with less sputtering than most of us; they have realized that everything is relative.

And that contest editor, ridiculous as he may look, deserves more respect than he would if he had taken her retelling merely because his stenographer told him that it was a Chekhov story and Chekhov was world-famous. Preferring the inferior shows healthier taste than piously applauding what is "supposed to be great." Crude taste grows more exacting if it encounters higher satisfactions. Coarse fingers squeezed into exquisite gloves do not become sensitive. So, let's put up with obtuse repudiations as tolerantly as we do the usual refined amens.

But how about plot? Does civilization outgrow plot? Does plot belong with the "solitary horseman" and survive today for tots and toddling intellects? Well, it's just about as out of date as war.

For the same reason. Clash, conflict, opposition are in everything from bird against the wind to Allies against the Axis. The interest of life is in the struggle. It is in little moments of wriggling by, of barely overtopping opposition. In such play rise all the drama and all the stories.

To you it might be exciting to see a tiny sapling birch slowly lift a ten-pound rock. You may marvel at the way a jack-in-the-pulpit stalk pushes up a foot-square mat of gray-brown leaves. A major earthquake destroying a great city makes a real impression on someone else. And so it is with plot. Simple-subtle and expansive in suggestion or complex-obvious with meaning on the surface, a story must have a push up or a turn. And the good writer will write stories with his sort of bursting through or of turning frustrations into fulcrums.

The greatest stories will be those which have most power of taking readers around a turn. A quiet unexaggerated story, with the rhythms that you find in daily life, can carry you around a corner and show your town, your home, your job, as chances for adventure. Or one can swing you around a curve to where the thing you always shunned bursts on you, sad and funny, not too dangerous to be loved.

To make the reader's heart leap up or to give him a twinge he never quite forgets, a turn is stronger than a revolution. The turn of a hair can be enough, or the mocking turn to crimson of a frost-struck sumach bush. But, if we think we have outgrown the big-tent, three-ring stories with happy endings, shall we prefer "all lived wretchedly until the revolution"? The newer, more sophisticated falsity still assumes the old. It assumes that one big turn can take us where we can enjoy success without a struggle, delight without danger, or security without shutting out the air.

Stories in which all mankind are merely victims are as dully false as the rides of the Lone Ranger. It takes some affirmation or some resistance to make a story.

But don't decide to concoct plots. Don't get cynical and decide to "give them what they want." In every good story the author believes what the story as a whole implies. The author of *Aesop's Fables* probably did not believe that animals talk. But he believed the implications. You may want a more complete illusion than allegory affords, but authenticity is not enough unless you, too, imply.

If nothing comes to you pointing toward a possibility because someone turns a corner or a hair, then go for a walk.

XXVII

A poem is more times distilled

POETRY is of so many kinds that almost anything you say of it is wrong. And if you get to concentrating on the kinds you like the best—and look for much more of—you get a shock, turning pages of anthologies: half the definition in your head does not apply. Desire to be fair and thorough ties your tongue. You cannot, however, continue speechless; the kinds of poetry you do admire seem so important, you have to champion them. And so you unloose the member that is certain to missay. Your truth will be tainted. Facts, preferences, and desire will intertwist and blend. And what you declare *is* may be almost half the rarely realized possibility.

So beware. Make the allowance you have to, when I say poetry and mean the poetry I like best and the poetry I want young friends of mine to write. If you listen to or read what people think of poetry you have to take it with your wits about you and your grains of salt, or else you have to take such platitudes as I shall state and have done with in the following fourteen points.

1. Poetry is generally akin to music, in using sounds and making its appeal partly to the ear. The sounds may be sounds of song, sounds of oratory, sounds of almost pure emotion—moans and delighted hums—or sounds of, obviously or not so obviously, impassioned speech.

2. Though the most abstract, the most conceptual, the most philosophical and the most technological language has been and is being used in poetry, the language of

poetry is, even on the mud flats, given its motion by emotion. The emotion ranges from apathy to zest. It ranges from ennui, that barely misses inanity, to ecstasy.

3. In general, poetry is more intense than prose. Inferior poems use once intense language for mild feeling. Great poems often make hitherto mild language for the first time intense.

4. Poetry is generally more concentrated than prose. Each syllable, each image, each rhythm, each pattern of rhythms may function in from two to n ways at once.

5. Poetry is generally more physical in its material, in its promptings, and in its operation than prose.

6. Poetry is generally more subtle, more complex, more vague, and more spiritual than prose.

7. Poetry ranges from the nonintellectual, as in "Hickory, dickory, dock," to the superlatively intellectual, as in "Here we go round the prickly pear" and adjacent lines. It tends, take all history and all varieties of poetry into account, to circumvent the intellectual, realizing without formulas and tracing a curve from nonsense to man's most inclusive wisdom.

8. Poetry is close to the animal snort and coo.

9. Poetry is close to either God or the ultimate vacuum without a wall.

10. Poetry is liked by children, barbarians, and the most mature.

11. Poetry includes, and has always been a safety valve for, the wildest eccentricities.

12. Poetry is riddled with, ridden by, and largely a dependent of tradition. See William Butler Yeats's edition of contemporary poems, *The Oxford Book of Modern Verse,* 1936, and *The Poets of the Year.*

13. Poetry is one of the chief human functions that, like language itself, bind hundreds of generations of humanity together. In some poetry, tradition is alive.

14. Full comprehension of poetry is usually difficult, either because it is more complex than you or because it gives shape to an achieved simplicity beyond your present growth. Sometimes, only because technique is elaborated in lieu of meaning.

But you see I am beginning to cheat. I might as well stop trying to evade either my conscience or my prejudice.

Now do not allow any of these platitudes about poetry, the congenital and implacable foe of platitude, to deter you from writing verse. However, if they do, poetry is not the loser; for poetry rises from desires that "will find out the way."

The desires that give rise to poetry grow stronger if they are pent. And you need not be loath to hold your verses back to "fill with ripeness to the core." You have probably had experience of holding your desires till you can satisfy them more completely than most of us have the guts for, after a little frustration. Repression can multiply your power.

The best poem is no petal. It is a fruit. It is a nut. It is a mature seed.

XXVIII

You pull yourself together
—or imagine

Do not try to write a poem until you want to. And when the spur pricks the side of your intent, do not get scared and strain at the composing. There will be a time for labor. But do not, at first, get busy with the systematic part of your mind. Your materials are long since gathered. Let us hope that they come from far and wide, from recently and long ago, and that not too many came from books.

Let us, further, hope that, apart from all your sorted and filed knowledge, you have a cellar and an attic and numerous catchall cubby holes, forgotten remnant bags, and boxes full of pieces, parts, and scraps. And, one hope further still, let us hope that your unclassified possessions were not kept because they once reminded you of scenes and characters, poetic themes, and attitudes in books. You are lucky if the thing that caught your eye, the thing you thought might some day come in handy, and the thing you brought home, unnoticed, entangled like a twig of bramble, were all too slight or common to have a literary stamp.

Obviously these treasures are both words and usages and things of touch and sight. They are bits of action. They are revealing turns of speech. They are intonations and inflections that go with feeling things a certain way. And the heft of things, that you know by carrying and lifting with your back, the hang of things like violins and crosscut saws and a catboat helm in a squall, the smell of shower bath water from an unused pipe, the rub of dry palmettos on your cheek, the cool feel of water from a special bubbling spring where fern fronds hang: you must have treasured up a million such particulars.

Knowing that your store is copious, you can use them sparingly. And sometimes one for the eye, one for touch or tension will come together, by some relatedness never known before, and in turn call up the emotion-carrying sounds.

But perhaps you are entirely a city person. Too bad, but never mind. You have people everywhere: babies, business men, bus drivers, scrub ladies, undertakers, aldermen's wives, and cranks. You have heard a lot of talk, some of it impassioned, along dark corridors and over two-party telephones. You have seen mildew and roaches, dogs and flies. Sometimes the sun reflects against a windowpane. There are many sorts of clouds. Probably as a matter of fact there are parks as well as parkways. Concrete and machines cannot conceal growth and change. And you, too, have your materials.

Something has jarred you, filled you with a vague hankering or elation, or put you in a state. Gradually your emotion takes a shape without a name, a kind of hungry hollowness that becomes magnetic. All sorts of feelings stir. Covers slowly lift, doors swing ajar, and the memories that answer gather in the hole. Like iron filings in a magnetic field they drag and jump to place, until the vagueness has grown to a design.

You have the configuration, then, for your part of the poem. And it has a magnetism of its own. Sounds and syllables rush from lurking places to fit their appropriate memory and feeling, and take their part in the design. And, now, your consciousness reinforces or counteracts a little. There is more danger of too much interference than of not enough. But your point of view is in full play, as it must have been when you brought your treasures home. It rejects, accepts, and waits until, suddenly, you have a rhythmic line, or possibly a stanza, of your poem.

Then there is a harder and more exciting kind of matching to be done. You still have to match words and sounds and modulations to the image where the magnetic hollow was; now you also have to match or balance the line or stanza you have made. It may be torture, but when the right match and contrast asserts itself you have your compensation, and more too.

The suspense and the fulfillment will be caught in the structure of your verse. Perhaps you held off the answering rime or assonance until, when it arrived, it gave exactly the right relief and the right stretching of the tentacles for more. And you may, in fidelity to the original hollow indication, leave something to be desired.

For what you have, though a finished performance as far as you control, is but the negative. What happens in the reader makes the final positive. And it may be that in your next composing you can have energy to spare in a little more heed to helping him. To think about the reader's part too much will spoil all. But let us take a chance.

XXIX

To wake the dormant poet in your reader

WHILE YOUR POEM is gathering and forming, you have no free attention for your reader. All you are is focused on collecting and composing to fit the shape of your present meaning. This hollow ache toward form sucks all your energy, the way a cyclone does the air. And all your thought is the gradual condensing and relating of experience-stuff that will take the shape of, and give living substance to, the thing you mean. That form, your poem, is going to liberate and make effectual a thousand frustrate impulses. They have partly devoured each other. They have embraced and coalesced. This time you will do a deed.

But no. The magnitude of the effect will be almost indiscernible. And to act its minikin action your poem must have at least one reader. And he must do more than nod, smile, or praise. He must inversely recapitulate, though partially and dimly, the whole cycle of experience of which your words upon the page become the sign. He must take on, as a radio receiver does the music or the voices from the electric waves, the pattern of rhythm and the images, and from them and manipulated by them, himself take the composition of desires and realizations which formed the poem. To reach an action your poem must, finally, go out, crossed with meaning different from your own, in actions of the reader.

Nothing short of such a process can justify the imaginative person for being, so much of his time, other than a man of action. A quite successful poet would be a person who accepted his constitutional impediments to engineering, producing wealth, and governing because, if you gave him time, he would accomplish more for the common health, well-being, and delight, through people that he moved.

But there are no quite successful poets. No quite successful poets any more than there is a quite successful God. Both have abundant occasion for despair—or humor.

If you know, inside, that you can be a poet, you will cherish no illusions. In their place will grow an indissuadable and humorous resoluteness and gradual resolution. "All but imperceptible effects" will be all you ask. And you will get your greatest fun in growing competent to produce that merest trace.

You may be smiling, still, at what I so solemnly declared must happen in a reader. All right. I know, at last, the interpretation of that smile. You smile, but you will not content yourself with less, though your achievement be sad-comical. You will not deceive yourself, not even if all authoritative voices call you greatest, just before you die. Acclamation, fullest recognition, exciting and requiting though they are, will not suffice. What you want and, unless you are ruined by success, will always want is to do your deed. And that, you know quite well, depends on real response.

Response is what I so extravagantly described. It is a shaping to the shape you offer, by another. And you want as much as possible of such response. You want many readers. But you care most about the readers who, for your moment, inwardly and totally respond. You are glad of readers who, for all sorts of reasons—compulsion, fashion, superficial pleasure—read you. Some of these will make you known to one that you can truly move. A few, against their wont, will themselves be moved. But the readers that you count are those who, a little because of you, see, feel, understand, effectually desire.

And, now that we agree that much, what can I suggest that the poet do about it? I have spent a paragraph insisting that a possessed writer can have no mind to spare for audience. Is this just another creek I say that you are up?

Certainly. And yet I have also insinuated that the more creeks you are up, the better you know geography. The more creeks you are up, the more you will risk on your ability to portage, swim, and shoot the rapids.

Your ability to do, with the imagination of the reader, what teachers sometimes do with tiny fists and pencils, what coaches do with enthusiastic athletes, what sergeants do with rookies—make the rookie walk and stand and breathe their way—is more a matter, I admit, of what you are than of what you see to.

Starting with the part that is mainly luck—and recognizing luck and using it is no small fraction of intelligence—you have much in common with many potential readers. No matter how nearly unique you are, no matter how defective you were born, in important ways you have much in common. Has your military experience or being a bandage-folder or auxiliary fireman helped you to grow up enough to thank God for all you still possess and are, in common with the common run?

Let us be obvious and list some common stuff. You may be a hunchback, clubfooted, blind in one eye, exceptionally neurasthenic, slow in reaction time, badly co-ordinated, very shy, too tall or obese; no matter what your handicaps, you once wore diapers. You now wear skirt or pants. Let us hope you have desire apparently suited to your garments. You surely have four or five primary desires, you have frustrations, you have many crude emotions; so has everybody else. You have had birthdays, bumps and big surprises, had frights and fights, been a fool and a misfit. So have all the rest of us. You are going to die. So are we all. Such are the communion elements that you can avail yourself of in the un-self-conscious effort for response. If you don't care about the sharing, there is grim, grave justice in the slightness of response.

If you like to eat but keep low interests from the higher and supposedly more poetic levels of your being, there is a division in you. And nothing alienates us from our fellows more than feeling superior to ourselves. We can be alone enough without being alien. And loneliness we have in common with all the world. You are, at best, but more courageous in not huddling to conceal it. And, if you decline to huddle, you want real meeting; you need your common humanness to induce readers to imagine what you write.

If, using all you share with them, you charm readers to compose with you, you will be doing more than giving pleasure and winning fame; you will be increasing the reader's flexibility and confidence for composing by himself. You will strengthen the heart of man against the grim inertia of his mechanisms.

XXX

We need some poets whose hair is
neither long nor overslick

MOST CURRENT VERSE is crestfallen. For more reasons than one, you would think some mutually praised poets fed on bromides. The fashion note in poetry is sounded by the dust that falls from crumbling bones. Trained listeners strain their ears for the nuance of nightingales' "droppings on the shroud."

Something has got into a few good poets' hair, and scores of docile followers try rubbing it on theirs. And of the two elixirs, drawn from the slightly shrunken fruit that elementary geographers used to say is like an apple, the oil of dejection has always flowed more copiously than any genuine oil of gladness. What is surprising is that so many new poets know so little history and poetry; they think they soak their heads in a new sump.

Mixing all the juices makes men's hair stand up. And most of the world's best poets have worn neither long love-locks nor hair so smoothed that healthy people want to frowzle it; they have had it mussed by their own hands fumbling as they made things go together in their minds. Their persevering and preternatural confidence, as it were, erects a cockscomb.

We look for poets whose hair can stand up. And we have poets who have not been refined beyond the power to bristle. A few can flaunt a menace with their manes.

Did anyone ever tell you not to get your dander up?

Well, which shall it be, dander or white feather? The thing to do with evil is keep on hating it, not prate of it.

But let your hair alone, except for normal comb and scissors. And don't shy from companionship with poets who managed to face a world as hard for them as yours for you, and still to have good times. Try poets like the anonymous author of "The Cherry Tree Carol," who knew the mischief that must be in divinity and had the infant Jesus pipe, within his mother's womb, "See, Joseph, she hath cherries at command." Read Shirley's "Death the Leveler," the "Sceptre and crown must tumble down" poem, to see virtue and the certainty of death honestly played with. Read Suckling. Read "Shall I, wasting in despair." Read Donne when irony makes his spirits rise the higher. Read Burns's "Tam o' Shanter," Emily Dickinson's hopscotching in the graveyard sunshine, Hardy's triolet, "Winter in Durnover Field," D. H. Lawrence's poems of animals, Sandburg's "Four Preludes on Playthings of the Wind," anything by Robert Frost, and John Crowe Ransom's "The Three Mountebanks."

But, mostly, get away from those writers who are involved and embroiled in the particular presentation of the future that is bothering you. Go back to Chaucer, who is a better craftsman than you think, and, though not utterly mature, closer to wholeness functioning than most writers have yet come. And go back to what disheartens you. Defy it. Get after it. Maybe you can get haired up this time, and never "cease from mental fight" and yet know the fight as "a lover's quarrel with the world."

XXXI

To keep abreast of worse than thorns,
of more than the times

Arnold Winkelried, at the battle of Bicocca in 1522, ran alone against the advancing enemy. He made a breach, that his exhilarated comrades could rush through, by grasping all the spears his arms could reach against his breast. A poet might do more than fling himself upon the thorns of life and bleed. If bleeding is inevitable, why let the blood merely drip and drizzle?

One who meets life's sharp and pressing points with confidence need not pay attention to poetic fashions. He will be discovering what is newer than brand new. What is brand new must have been invented long enough ago to have been granted patent, to have stock taken in it, and to have had the brand designed or sewed or stamped. You had better be an unbranded poet, who makes something of all that hurts, delights, and baffles him, forming for himself and showing others how to be form-makers.

If your youth is renewed like the eagle's you will always have the potential of newness with you and you can never tell where it will dazzle. Your trouble, when young, will not be dearth of newness. It will be confusion. But that is to the good if you are thoroughly confused and explainers cannot quiet your quandary. You will pull yourself together, over and over. Resilience is one thing that being a poet requires.

And common things intensely experienced and composed with some come-uppance are always new. If you feel a shoot of joy as you catch sight of small gold droplets in the grass and weeds out where you go to dump the waste, do not disdain the feeling. You don't know your gold by suitability for jewelry or coins. And it was not there last night. It roundly holds the sun to the green of earth, shaped water out of the air.

Such little sights may save you from running up and down the beach to keep abreast of the tide. You know of changes that do not leave things the more as they were before, the more they change. And the way you will breast the sea of life is swimming. Sometimes you may lie upon the changing, changeless sea, face upward, floating under stars that seem to wink.

XXXII

And constantly come close to
full composure

THE BEST of poets point beyond their reach. And as long as they are playing their part in the comitragedy that the rest of us are cast in, they will reach toward integrity without forgetting the duality represented by two legs, two arms, two ears, two hemispheres of brain. If, like Æ, they write sometimes as if they had reached the One and left the Many, they will at those times leave us, too.

You are lucky if, wanting to write a poem, you still strongly feel the common person's suspicion of the ethereal. Most contemporary verse writers, except the plainly unintelligent, abhor the ethereal and equally the etherizing. In that abhorrence our times are definitely up a level from the century before and many other centuries. In that one way nearly all our poets who are good at all are nearer to the peaks. But most stay far beneath the great poets. Their honesty is at the expense of humorless self-pity, of dryness. Many of them are seduced by systems—political, philosophical, or aesthetic systems. They have ceased to experience the inexplicable. They are insulated in oversimplifications, like people who know the weather only through the glass walls of an air-conditioned modern house.

For there are two kinds of adult simplicity, at opposite human poles. One is the simplicity of insusceptibility; it may be due to native dullness, or it may be due to too much credulity toward intellectual formulations. The other kind of simplicity human beings can but approach. It would be incorporating all the paradoxes.

Most of us, with all our might, have gone no farther than Koheleth, the author of the sad, lovely book, misplaced in the Bible, the Book of Ecclesiastes. But the beginning place for poetry that is greater still, the only place for energetic minds to start their answering from, is where Koheleth stopped: "Vanity of vanities, all is vanity and a sighing after wind." The best poets see what Koheleth saw; they feel none the less that there is more than vanity for man, and, at length, holding fast and firm the feeling which undeniable delight burned into them, they produce the evidence. Though all things change and pass, yet the joy, strength, and understanding, the generous affection and the courage to keep shaping forms of order in the flux never lose their value. The best poets prove that what plies between the flux and the illusory world of clock and calendar can never disappear. Imagination mocks at vanity, laughs at locks and clocks, and newly achieves significance.

If you ask for specific illustration of wisdom that goes beyond Koheleth in honesty and inclusiveness, turning despair into creative resolution, I give you, now, as in a toast, Shakespeare's *King Lear*. I give you, to be still more specific, though remembering that the whole play is truer than any component, the characters Kent and Edgar as seen in the entire fabric of relations. I know no greater poem—yet. I know several hundred that imply a congruous resolution. One ends:

> Let us roll all our strength and all
> Our sweetness up into one ball,
> And tear our pleasures with rough strife
> Through the iron gates of life.
> Thus, though we cannot make our sun
> Stand still, yet we will make him run.

To such a poet, the way things seem is important. It is not enough. He strives to make them seem and be the same. He partly reconciles the world of clock and calendar with the world that his delights and dreams disclose. "We will make him run." He momentarily imposes form on flux. And within the untoward circumstances, under the adverse conditions, at the never quite propitious time, he briefly achieves natural and ordered freedom. He proves the possibility by what he does in the small action of composing a poem: turning limitations into implements, using the beat of time to indicate ways to make time yield us joy. In a poet who can make our sun serve man's desire, modernity and history converge. Animality and nobility get within the span of outstretched fingers. And science and religion taper towards a point.

But the poet cannot claim to reach the fusing apex. He says, "The visible flame wavers and turns invisible before the converging margins unite." And so the best of reconcilers never quite achieves the composure that perhaps is God's.

In a spiral he aspires. His work remains the frustum of an upward cone.

XXXIII

The novel writer has more rope

WE DON'T HAVE our eyes open very long before we discover that we could do and have things now impossible to us, if we were older. But before long we *are* older and we discover that we have lost something. No one now is quite so concerned that we should be safe and happy as when we lacked the privileges of sitting up late and making plans without asking for permission. We are not liked, any more, because we are cute and little and dependent, and our own folks get ruffled at the signs that we have memories, minds and wills that diverge from theirs and vigorously assert themselves. Things are expected of us and we are held responsible. We begin to realize faintly that there is no great gain without what we, for a while, choose to call some small loss. After a good many more years of living, that faint realization, which, for a long time, we supposed was relevant to only a few matters in our individual experience, begins to apply to more and more of hope and expectation; not only to personal but family, political, educational, and all human hopes. And now the loss may seem, in unilluded moments, equal to the gain. We have begun to feel what Samuel Johnson called *The Vanity of Human Wishes*. And it shows a certain toughness of fiber in us if we realize the perception clearly. We have begun to mature.

But another toughness in us is tenacious of a sense of value in our efforts, a sense of something solidly amassed, in the exchange of gains and losses. It will not tolerate a too complete assent to the indisputable proposition that you can't eat your cake and have it, too. There is, we know, a silliness and a cowardice in not admitting it. There is, we feel, a catch, a flaw, an irony, that makes it false, and still more craven, to bow our heads and hearts and let it go at that.

With both toughnesses at work, and working opposite, within us, we have our silly ups, our whipped and spiritless downs. And yet our exhilarations are not all fatuous, our dejections not all feeble. Effects of deep delight last through depressions. We are on the way to becoming more mature. And we keep looking.

We look for people who do not content themselves with having just a bigger pile of shavings at their feet, a dwindling stick in their hands under the whittling knife. And we find them. The shavings are deep around their shoes, but what they hold is, we get to see, a rude but lovely, strong, mocking, daring, almost shaped figure. The figure, though it certainly was once a stick of wasting wood, is full of something more than potential shavings. It indicates, implies, curves and rises and is firm; something animates it. More than wood, something in the shape asserts, by being, that inexpressible small irony we felt: something has come to be, that was not in the stick of wood, that is not in the shavings.

Such people, when we find them, whittling more than shavings, are not in all ways less young because they are older. They are not less determined because they have often failed. They are not unfeeling because they have listened to reason, and "submitted to unreason." They are not inflexible though they are disciplined. They are not insensitive though they are robust. They do not stop caring for kindliness and mutual assistance, for give-and-take and reliable and thorough work, because they perceive in themselves and all of us fears, jealousies, and foolish pride that almost cancel out our generous sentiments and wishes. They are not sterile even though they have experienced many deaths. They are not devoid of faith because they find evil inextricable from living. They can smile and be at ease, hold command and be precise and thorough, take risks and accept setbacks, and vigorously enjoy, though they sympathize intensely with others' pain and misery, suffer on their own part more chagrins and maimings than less unyielding people, and go always further into forbidding mysteries, which they know already that none can ever fully comprehend.

Finding other people who (though manifestly and often most distressingly weak, foolish, and pathetic, somewhere in their lives and actions) do carve a figure instead of vainly whittling away a stick gives us the corroboration that we need for making a life instead of wasting, bitterly and sourly, between fatuous dreams and futile busy work.

And novels as well as poems reveal such people, behind the figures that they make. If you write such a novel you bake a cake that we can eat and always partly have.

Two such people are Jane Austen with *Emma* and *Persuasion,* and Tolstoy with *Anna Karenina* and *War and Peace.* You or any bright sophomore can find faults with any of these novels. And greater may be written. I am not going to say more about them here than that in them, as in a few flesh and blood people, I have beyond doubt seen the stick of wood become the immortal form. As indications that human beings can do more than vainly whittle with their accidental knife and stick of wood they are among the most convincing.

There is no point in attempting to determine whether novels of their power are as great as poetry by equally unbeaten people. You write what you are good at, what offers you the most alluring challenge. Or like Thomas Hardy, Melville, and Goethe, you write in two or three kinds and have your fullest joy and fullest power in one.

The play of forces, the wave length of vibration, the amplitude of possible inclusiveness appear less restricted in the novel; it is the only epic so far successful in our day. But if you are a poet you will feel that the little seed is quite as powerful as the collected waters giving back the energy that lifted them at Grand Coulee dam.

For better or for worse, the novel shares the weakness of the flood. Its widespread, startling copiousness is mainly superficial and it cannot change the landscape as seeds do every spring.

But if you are to be a novelist, you will hope for more than the usual thousand copies, and will say, "I will touch many people a little, giving them an hour of being much alive, and maybe with a few I can really mesh, a little while." You may extract juice from almost everything you touch. Your modesty may hold you back from thinking of any deep importance in your work, and you may try to brush aside all thought of influence, declaring that many things, that happen and are, interest you, may interest us, and that is all. If modesty is not shirking responsibility, all right.

An enthusiastic old Irish-American, little by little, told me the story of his life, the other day. And every once in a while he capped an incident by saying, "I'm telling you. That is the way life is." He did not know it, but he was trying to influence me. His story was warm and human, full of fight, shock, loyalty, enterprise, and pathos. Once I would have said—suppose someone made his narrative a novel—"If it is interesting and makes you feel 'such is life,' then it is good." But the protest all have heard so many times has now more weight with me: "Oh, we get enough of that all the time; we do not want just what experience gives us every day." The good novel meets the challenge. It shows things as they are but implies whatever it is *in* things as they are that for the writer makes life interesting to live.

Famous writers have not always been clear about what kept them interested and adventurous. Thackeray, for instance, thought it was mostly pity and ironic amusement, and, like so many writers in our tradition, his treatment of the good women and the Dobbins let out the ambiguous cat: you might be good if you could not be smart. He never clarified his tenderness, and so he clung with feeble feeling to what intelligence could not respect. The compassionate yet ironic feeling makes us love him, however inadequate it was to cope with his disgust and indolence and clarify the thinking. Dickens never let the denizens of his glorious Dickens world, with all its rich abundance and hilarity, be as individually complex as actual people are. And virile Fielding could not trust the mangled virtue that was in his own deeds as magistrate; to keep a plea for goodness he poured virtue, thick and sticky, on his Sophias and Amelias and hewed out by rationalistic ethics the wooden image of Squire Allworthy.

These great writers are more masterly than most of those who see their faults, and it would be well to read them until we have more who can succeed where they failed.

Balzac illustrates ranging intelligence. He shows the novel full of impassioned people, whipping up thick realness with their impacts and counter acts. The width and height a novel affords he used to create a dense, atmosphere-charging play of motive and event. It was heroic creation. The human race has potentialities less crushable than Goriot, less mean than Rastignac. Few novelists have misrepresented less than Balzac; strength and sweetness in real people are sometimes better mixed.

And even Flaubert: he is able to give us sensuous experiences that relate and correlate, until the whole life of

Emma Bovary is substantial in our imaginations, with all her associates three-dimensional and yet seen through. We see, we understand. There is no one that we like. Something failed in Flaubert's temperament; something is not allowed for in his point of view.

Thus it is with most great novelists. With all their fertility, their disciplined fidelity to fact, the great variety of experiences they draw from, and the opportunity that the medium provides for keeping readers watchful as motives and circumstances ply and thrust and twine, few can give both the little and the larger truth. The very magnitude of their attempt betrays the one or two ways, among the many needful, in which they did not manage to compose.

But herein lies your opening. You can learn to accept and set your limits, suit your extensiveness to your capacity, and concentrate your composing to make sure that your sense of people, sense of fact, sense of humor, and sense of possibility all compose. If that takes half a lifetime and if that is all that you get in, you have enough. You have statuette as well as shavings. And you leave your statuette for those who will be looking when you are gone.

XXXIV

But you had better use experience,
not autobiography

It is what you have been through, yourself, that enables you to write a novel. But if you make yourself your subject the principal figure in your novel is likely to be least alive. You may be modest, or you may be vain, or you may be on the defensive. You may be leaning back hard against self-pity. You may, like one young novelist I knew, be so determined not to be a hero that you eventually think you have to insert sugary interludes to relieve the gruff-and-grim account. You are not likely to leave all the obvious and subtle forces of your character free and in their characteristic setup of checks and balances.

Pretty normal people, when they write a story from their literal experience, usually assume that their own tastes or motives are *the* natural ones. They take so much for granted that the reader cannot, little by little, deposit from his own desires, sensations, and emotions in the outlined character so that the character fills out and stands and moves, and is a person.

Besides, attempts to examine with detachment one's own present or recent configurations of sensation, impulse, and response are never quite successful. You may protest that you can look at yourself without prejudice. Are you sure that, if you do, you are not twisting a tourniquet somewhere in your circulation?

If you have been given, much, to introspection, you must have had the experience that Cardinal Newman shockingly describes. You must sometimes have felt like one, looking straight before him into a mirror, who sees nothing but the blank and shining glass. It is seldom quite so bad as that. But if you are all there looking in how can you be all there, inside, to be watched?

We can have all sorts of conceptions of ourselves. We never know the particular outward manifestations and their correlation with guessed-at inner states which set up irritations, commiserations, and even admirations and affections in the people who look upon us from outside. We may partly see and try to guess. That, of course, we often do. But nearly always we are partly wrong.

Too many autobiographic novels have been liked and

had an influence, however, to insist that autobiographic novels will not do. But the important paradox is that, though it is yourself and your own life you know, the way to use that knowledge most undistortedly and freely is by putting yourself in living people's places, and un-self-consciously realizing what they feel.

If sympathetic imagination is always saving you from saying, "I don't see why," "I can't understand," and "Why on earth did she—," then always you are gathering wherewithal for dramatic presentations. The inner and the outer stay for you in dynamic relation, like the swinging bell and bell tongue and the sound. You won't have to explain motives. You can show us the behavior and let us—erroneously—feel that the insight is our own.

You know the feelings that go with acts you never did, because you almost took the choice that led that way, some time ago. Your characters are, many of them, people who, 'way back, took one horn of a dilemma that you had to seize by both. All the choices that you never made, because you could not forfeit the satisfaction nor forego the fun attached to either side, now furnish you with sympathies on both the sides. And what had made you a little uncomfortably detached now enables you to identify yourself with many sorts.

The characters that a writer convincingly creates are people the like of whom, "if he had chosen," he almost might have been. Jane Austen doubtless caught a strand of her own mind, at some time, running like the silly Mrs. Bennet. And Shakespeare had seen Falstaff, Iago, Beatrice, and Coriolanus in himself. And you, too, can contain multitudes. Perhaps you have a certain gentleness toward the mean, the conventional, and the hysterical, because you remember times when, but for the tenacity of a single hair or the grace of God, you might have been that way. Perhaps you can sympathize with both crook and convert. You need to "inwardly know" all the unlike kinds you want to create, as George Eliot knew both Maggie Tulliver and Dinah Morris, as Hardy knew all three, Clym Yeobright, Wildeve, and the Reddleman, as Turgenev knew both Bazarov and the fathers of the older generation.

This inclusiveness—indecision of character, as it probably looks to serious aunts when the future novelist is young—this being many kinds of person, though it disqualifies him as a specialist, also takes him further in the know of substances and living things, of practices, processes, and characteristic ways and customs than one who settles down too earnestly and circumspectly to systematic business ever gets. His sensuous experience may not make him quite an expert in oystering or ways of doing hair; it furnishes him with smells and motions, the names of tools and tricks of handling that no mere systematic person could possess in half so many fields.

The more you know, the less you will need to be literal about your own private story. And I suggest that you write of selves you might have been, and people you can find yourself in, but not about yourself till you are dead.

XXXV

Even criticism can be imaginative

"Everyone is queer but thee and me. And thee is a little queer." We need yardsticks; we need some impersonal criterion. But yardsticks will not measure manifold motion. On earth there can be no agreed-upon criterion applying to that which plies between the calendared fictions and the flux behind the clock and calendar. "Concerning taste disputation is vain (it ought not to be disputed)." Is good taste, then, a vacuous phrase? Or is taste a sort of bogey in which few of us believe but which most of us will consent to call up when we take offense?

Mussolini and Hitler attempted to cancel the personal and to eliminate relativity. Mussolini stood upon the shores of change with ax and whipping rods. Hitler restored a rectilinear wheel as his Kampf symbol. And millions, scared of relativity, hoped for a little whip, a little chance to hear screamed proofs of their own power from beneath their own small chariot wheels. They welcomed, or cautiously wondered about the efficiency of, the new order.

But too many people in the world still expected to get a little power without handing a dictator the end of a rope, noosed around their own necks. And on the side of the Allies, with them, fought the smaller number who find it fun to live and let live. In peacetimes these few rely on force that is the more potent because, for many, it is occult: the force of the spirit, a curious distillate of nerve and body force.

But even the freedom-lover, let him accept the twentieth-century guise of Protean relativity as cheerfully as self-trust and faith make possible, even he would like a rating on his work.

In the long run he will get it, relatively but surely, with the rough justice of this universe. He will get it from the market. He will get it from the lip-praise of those who praise what others praise. He will get it, indirectly, from the unintentional respect shown by authoritarian critics, who, like minnows, always move in schools. He will get it from scattered corroborating readers, a few in each of many generations, and from the genuine critics.

You suppose "genuine critic" means one who agrees with the writer? Yes; you have something there. I promise to give a fuller definition. But, first, let us try to understand the sort of critics between whom and you I should like to put a stumbling block.

They are too sensitive to accept the most familiar way of meeting the difficulty of the personal equation. They were once too much alive to cope with relativity by leaving all but things in sight alone. They could not live by violence, kept usually where a policeman keeps his night stick, nor ignore in themselves and others all desires and feelings that would make them different.

(I once saw that majority solution articulated as it seldom is. In a score of freshman autobiographies, more than half the boys kept saying, "There is nothing special about me. I do what other boys of the right sort do, not well enough, except in athletics, for my neck to stick out, and I feel what they feel, assume what they assume. Just a regular, healthy American young man, whose father is doing well, I hope to have a lot of fun in college, study enough to pass, and, when I get my degree, settle down to bossing people, getting married, going to church, and being a success.")

The future authoritarian critic despises such conventional compromise. He starts as one of us, the slightly dubious sort who read this book. He not only takes Einstein, Heraclitus, and Koheleth seriously; he feels relativity around and in himself. But is there not some special area, like his nook among the library stacks, in which select but unaggressive people can have an order, of the mind?

In the better universities and colleges he eventually discovers a cadaverous kinsman among the more brilliant young professors. No warmth is encouraged. But there is phosphoric light. After a while a smoldering heap of embers is uncovered in the ashes. He learns that *mores* are for the herd. But there is an ethic, for the disciplined. And there is an aesthetic for those who are intellectual enough to keep it unconfused. It requires a slow initiation, in which he puts off the personal. Or, if that is not quite possible, he expunges everything personal from his higher vocabulary. He learns that art is a thing by itself. Works deserving of consideration must be regarded for themselves, in themselves, bare of relation to a life, or life.

Thus the future critic will exempt himself, as critic, from relativity. He forms his mind on Form. And form is not, for him, a forming of experience; still less is it a forming for experience. It is form, pure. The pleasures of form are like the pleasures of mathematics, when the mathematician securely trusts that none of his formulas will ever be applied. Never admitting to himself the ego-flattery of such an exclusive kind of "expertise," the authoritarian critic acknowledges pure gratification, unsullied by enthusiasm, in recognizing the full *how* of structure, and the "mechanisms" that operate in an object of esteem.

Art, for him, is craftsmanship consummate, almost without relations, and enhanced by being surrounded by bewildering relativity. When he knows the *how* of several works, so generally accepted as masterpieces that they can, without suspicion, be assumed, then he can derive subtle standards, binding in the pure realm of form. Knowing the mechanisms and how they should be used, he can assay all new and lesser works.

The give-away of this solution by avoidance is inability to recognize new greatness. If someone neglects to use the learned components of the forms he has revered, neglects to compose with the mechanisms that he has earnestly analyzed, he is unable to discover form.

But he is having the serious say, today. And maybe his doctrinaire dogmatisms will find their function in the relative scheme of things and do little more harm than yesteryear's one-winged Marxian criticism, or the criticism that tries to be of all schools and praises everything. These last more numerous and less formidable critics save their faces, if not their full intelligence, by the reservation that of course not much contemporary literature will live. They leave "time" to do the close discrimination, and keep sedulously up with the times.

The genuine critic is the most obviously fallible of all. He may even learn more and change his mind. I can cite no perfect examples, and you, or I, would have important differences with each one. Mark Van Doren has written genuine, imaginative, and unpretentious criticism, in recent years; so have Virginia Woolf, Edmund Wilson, John Holmes, J. Donald Adams, Jacques Barzun, Mary Colum, and Lewis Mumford. There are a good many.

They stay in relativity, along with the things they like. They accept the complication of being persons. They keep on individually pulling themselves together, and respond to books and poems with all that in them is. They tacitly admit blind spots, ignorance, prejudices, and affections, and grow as honest as they can, with their limitations on their heads. They do not pretend that they can insulate literary values from interests, enthusiasms, and fears, but meet what they read with all they are, such as they are.

A genuine criticism shows a human being responding to an experience, and indicates as much as possible why his experience was what it was. It indicates how the experience temporarily disordered him; how, then, he found a way to order it. Then the reader responds to the criticism, making reservations and allowances.

The critic is not good taste. He is not good judgment. He is not abstract. He is a person who has delights, defects, and aversions. He should have matured imagination. We can tell by the way he writes how well composed he is, how deeply and coherently he has experienced. What he writes is one man making his comeback. Every word is what "I think," is "in my opinion." And if he is relative to enough, remembers his own relativity, and is yet composed, his critical composition is given with the authority of a shapely and still shaping life. None can have more authority.

XXXVI

What you write must be good
enough to sell

AMERICA is no place and the nineteen-forties is no time to be too high-thinking and fastidious for "money matters." Delegating dirty business is degrading. And, if our best imagination is to escape the taint of begging, it must know how its bread is buttered. Question begging is the least defensible beggary for a writer. Literature is not furbelows and bagatelles; it is comprehension and composition; it resolves what it can, with no ignoring.

A poet is a flunky unless he pays his way. Those who fondle the assumption that distinguished writing belongs only to a realm where the sordid clink of coins is never heard produce a thing that thoroughly hard-headed people would never buy, because it is a fake. To deserve to sell, it must be the perfected product of a person who has found a way to make of beauty and business a fertile cross.

What the Goulds and Hills of exploitation would prefer is, naturally, no interference. They can still be induced to foster libraries and writers, as they have the church, with the sly intention of keeping romantic fripperies and trade apart. They will buy what they can and pervert it to their own plans; what they cannot buy they will endow and segregate or sterilize. Kept to lofty and nonfunctioning purity, belles-lettres leave them free to multiply their power. That way they gain as much as if the writers took their orders.

But, if you are on the way to being a good writer, you may have realized that there are not many consistent and clear-scheming robber barons. Most men in business are a lot like you. What you have to say is meant for them. And if you develop the skill you can make some of them see much that you see, and be delighted and amused, a little moved. If they do like it they will want to pay, not an equivalent in cash for all its values, but a rough equivalent for the wages that your time and energy would have commanded in a job that you could have acquired the skills for, but would not have liked as well. If you cannot make people like your writing, while you are showing things that change their minds, you are not sufficiently the master of dilemmas to be paid.

From the point of view of the market your artistic integrity is, you must admit, a luxury. Any time, you are at liberty to come to your senses and show the world the world that is comforting to see. You do not have to sign with Mephistopheles. You can gradually see the way things operate in this world, make small, unclear, "necessary" adjustments, and, by small hedgings, come around. If you keep clear and refuse to "accommodate" yourself "a mite," that is your privilege; and, as our grandparents or great-grandparents used to say, "you have your reward." It would be unsporting to seize it and insist that you are a martyr, demanding pity from the world.

Should you be quite comfortable before a mirror if you caught yourself insinuating that all writers who sold their books and became widely loved belonged to the world, in an ignoble sense? Could you forget the sour grapes fable, when you knew that a nimbler wisdom and a tougher energy would have won you, too, the creative irony to belong and yet give your difference? For there are not only two alternatives: keeping your difference, with no function, and giving it up. The creative triumph is in giving it while you keep it.

And to give widely you have to sell. The universal suspicion of the thing to give away, "free, gratis, and for nothing," is well founded. Co-operation is good, and, when we are intelligent and mature, we shall have more of it. Yet not society alone but nature is also competitive. If you think man can use his full resources and co-operate only, watch a pair of two- and three-year-old babies with their toys, the best-loved, -nourished, and -pedigreed babies you can find. It would be worse than Solomon's proposal, with the halving sword, to eradicate the rivalry from either of them. Or keep your ears and eyes alert at any gathering of writers. (I do not charge that all are meanly vain or jealous. I know some who hardly deserve those epithets at all.)

Competition, though, is where the fun comes in. As usual the devil sneaks in, too, where there is fun. And sales, like votes, grades, degrees, awards, reputations, and positions, do not prove much. They do prove something. And they, paradoxically, prove much when they are got without compromise; when they are got by composing incompatibles.

Most professional writers are not genuine composers. Yet all genuine writers sooner or later become professional writers. (You may find an instance in which the money-taking was restricted to the heirs.) Neither Lord Byron nor Professor Housman succeeded in being exceptions. It is true that most professional writers take the dictates of the market; they satisfy an effectual demand. What you have to do, if you care too much to give the public what its merchants think it wants, is to give them what human nature, as represented by you, really hungers for, baffle their expectations with fascinating surprise, and get their money in token that you knew real wants.

With such an offering, enough times, at intervals, repeated, you will find an agent or a publisher upon whom you can work your legerdemain. For publishers are much like all the rest of us. And, in the squabbles between the so-called practical man and the so-called man of imagination, the publisher is sometimes the more generous and the more imaginative.

Do not call yourself a writer until you can include and shape enough to make a publisher and a public pay.

XXXVII

Rejections and delays can extend the life of what you ultimately write

YESTERDAY I scrutinized a hundred and ninety-three young orange trees. Most of them were waist-high, some breast-high, and a few rose just above my knees. On a few were blossoms; on many were buds about to open and tiny knots of white; and some had little, hard green threats of fruit. A handful of the buds were lousy—their petioles alive with small green lice; more were pure and shining. All I snipped and twisted off.

Whatever you may be thinking of an old man's sadism, the owner of the fruit farm asked me to. A well-bearing orange tree must have lived more seasons before it is allowed to crop.

After that, I went among the larger trees with small pruning shears and cut a thousand green shoots from trunks and lower limbs. Some brushed off, to leave a small, round green wound. Others, a little more fibrous, required scissoring blades, that met to part them from the wastefully luxuriant stem. And, as the curved jaws closed, a flush of green rushed up the sucker stalk, like a deep blush on a woman's neck. After many clippings a whiff from my moist fingers justified my thwartings of the trees: the sap that flowed in suckers might round mature fruit.

You do not have to be an habitual reader of the book supplements and reviews to know about the one-volume poets and the one-novel novelists. You do have to watch ten years or so to witness several instances of writers who have a flurry of fame as radicals and later become the perfume-squirters of those prosperous potentates who demand that well enough—for them—be let alone.

It would be falsely charitable to say they had matured, though what is commonly taken for maturity is knuckling under to the pretense that relativity relates only to the infinitesimally little and the astronomically large, and that the fabric of prevailing clockwise fictions includes all possibilities.

I told a father at Commencement, a few years ago, that his nineteen-year-old son, graduating with highest distinction, was the most mature new graduate I had known in twenty-five years of teaching. In depth and inclusiveness he was so much more mature than the father that it would have been wasting that able father's valuable time to unfold the evidence. And yet it is not sad that the son has achieved no recognition as a writer, yet. He wrote good poems in college. And his Commencement address on poetry deserved a place on the shelf of books on poetry with Shelley, Sir Philip Sidney, and Professor Saintsbury. But on the way home from the commencement exercises a secretary in a college office, the lively daughter of a member of the faculty, remarked loudly to her mother, "I did not understand a word he said." She spoke for many in that audience, including learned men, long intimate with the humanities, and definitely intelligent members of his class. And that insufficiency of the common touch is why it is not sad that one good young poet is not published yet.

Since graduating he has written more strong and simple poems, with rhythm and form all his own. But still it is not sad that he remains unpublished. For he was in the army from the beginning of the draft. As private, corporal, sergeant, he made friends with the assorted human beings of the draft; he won their confidence and a recognition, not only of himself by them, but, equally important, of them by him. As officer he made new and differently difficult adjustments. With all he learns, he keeps his sweet, mocking, humorous, and religious nature; he keeps, with small professions, his native and developed sap.

He may eventually write more richly, and of and for more people. His fruit should be ampler, with more ingredients in the juice, a still mellower assimilation of sun, snows and rains, and grit and mud of earth.

Some of us, for a long while, are disproportionately concerned about ways in which we differ from associates. We are conscious, painfully, of skills and gifts and graces that we lack. And, besides, things we care about are constantly in peril; we are not sure how hardy they may be, and over them we watch and brood, to the exclusion of much else that is also part of life. And, if we write, the subjects of our interest are consequently so special that even other highly individual people would find no interest in our stuff.

Yet one whose special quirk is product of strong desires and a few deep delights will not dicker for publication and approbation, even after many disillusions, by ironing out his meaning. He cannot damp his dangerous desires. He cannot acquire a scurf upon his quick. He writes because he is lonesome, but his loneliness will accept no substitutes. He must make a contact between the shy, striped, and crooked self and something corresponding in his readers. His individualness is a holding out for sociability that is real.

We have to learn, however, that real is never absolute. Otherwise we give up our marriages, withdraw from friendships, and become so terribly alone that our little self grows pallid like potato vines crawling in the cellar, withers to a dusty puffball, or shakes and shudders and throws itself away, in suicide.

And so I think it is lucky if slow success requires a writer to take a job and learn to get along with only partially congenial people. He may prove that co-operation without compromise will work. And he needs to know himself not only as the shy and subtle enthusiast but also as mere man, of so much bulk, such daily doings, such incomplete relations with other people. He needs to have the life of no one special, Jack or Bill, with an appetite and an accumulating record that would fill a paragraph in a dull obituary. (I congratulate all my talented young friends who wore uniform, lieutenant colonels, ensigns, sergeants, or buck privates.)

You need nearly as much bulk of cheap pine slats and uprights, or of stouter posts and crossbars, as of vine and sap and leaves, if you are to ripen flavorous grapes for many a palate. Whatever gives you more time and requires you to grow your commonness, while your specialness twines through and over it, is "a thing to thank God on," however vulgar, however stupid. For everything has its life significance, not in its belonging to the world behind the clock and calendar, alone, but in its power of mediating between the worlds on both sides of the clock. So, drink your tears and taste the common cup, when the self-addressed stamped envelope comes back.

XXXVIII

And in revising you become more adept in technique

YOUR MANUSCRIPT will have lost its immaculateness when it returns, and you may feel that it has wilted under careless eyes. It is still yours, but no longer part of you. Your hair on the barber's apron, to be shaken off and swept out of the way. But you had better toss it into a desk drawer. That is better than the wastebasket. You may sometime want to steal a good phrase from yourself.

More likely you will examine it as you would your hand when a bandage is removed. You see it more as a reader would than when enthusiasm was dilating your eyes. And, about the second page, you may come to a sentence that knits your brows. There were two possible ways a prepositional phrase might be taken, and, in reading, you had taken the one that spoiled the sense. You put in another comma. Or you draw a ring around the phrase and run an arrow to fit it in another place.

Further on, you run your pen through an intensifying adverb. The effect you got was of shrillness and not force. The adjective swims (stoutly) without the water wings.

On the next page you come to a noun qualified by two adjectives, and to replace all three another noun suggests itself. It does the work. This time you do not lay down your pen. You will tighten this thing up.

Presently you stumble at a sentence that runs in three directions, like little grass-fire flames on a day of fickle breeze. Everything said still seems important, and every clause and phrase clarifies the sense. With close attention, the unit meaning of the whole appears. It may be a branched candlestick, but it sheds a light. Each subordinate item helps to make the whole more true; each is interesting in itself. All it requires of the reader, after all, is that he put his mind to seeing unity in a thing that is complex. But no. No use in justifications; you were set back on your heels. You cannot ask the reader to believe that your unfocused sentence is worth the trouble. He has enough complexities of his own. Very well; you take the sentence apart. Part of it can make a following sentence. One clause can condense to an adjective. One qualifier you set one side. You may be able to get that in somewhere else. Another you ruthlessly discard. That is better. You have lost something. But you have gained more.

Then you read the passage over. It does not sound right. The sense is clear, but the rhythm is changed. In one place it goes completely dead. The feeling isn't there. Your fingers tighten to crumple the whole page.

But, inside you, the feeling that made you write the article or story is coming back. You relax your hand. Patching and pruning are not enough. But you cannot abandon the whole thing. It is absurd to care so much about a little realization and a lot of words. But you do care.

You get into a more comfortable chair and read the whole thing over. Paragraphs and pages please you. A forgotten phrase delights both ear and mind. You say it aloud. It is good, as if by some other writer. Like some happy bit of action that puts things to working right, it seems; not mere words.

You did not realize you were master of such technique. It must be a kind of grace that one is given if he feels what he is writing, strong and clear. And yet—you felt those earlier passages, that you changed. Not quite so concentratedly, perhaps. It would be wonderful, you think, if you could have the thing you want to write come firm and sharply outlined and then just set it down, and have it right.

Well, sometimes it does. But you would be luckier than human beings on earth can be, to have it always so. You would be altogether unified. But you would have lost your access to the changefulness of everything—the flux, that makes possible both error and kinetic meaning. You would be altogether of an existing order, no longer a pointer-out of possibility. And so you would be unlucky, too. Creation, large and small, risks the evil chance.

The best of writers have some things come whole and living, the first time, without a separate thought about technique. They avert the evil chance the whole way through, sometimes. But other things, eventually as fine, they labor over, keep, and little by little revise, until they are spontaneous and right. Probably you will do the same.

The danger is that you will let technique become too distinct. So you are probably fortunate if the time you think about it is when you look upon your product after it has cooled. And, after encountering difficulties of your own, you can hardly fail to learn from other writers' work. They have met like difficulties with success. You learn technique by identifying your imagination, for the time, with theirs. You find what you can do by doing it, first, with them.

If you also look into grammar, rhetoric, and more specialized treatments of technique, be sure you find the genuine masters, like the late Professor Jespersen; they treat words, versification, the short story, or the novel as variable, flexible, and relative. They will give not laws of the Medes and Persians but descriptions of changing usage. There are conventions, but the creative person takes the risk of choosing and combining, and twists the skein of usual and strange. He, still and always, plies between the clockwise, static round-and-round and the ever-flowing.

And you, you need to be alert, or all the possibilities you have discovered will be ignored in the ordered world. While revising, think about your reader, too. Keep remembering that it is his sensations and emotions that you work with, and that he will feel irrelevant emotions if you flaunt proprieties that he has learned with pains. You want to be sure you are not repelling. You don't want your reader to evade imagining and start questioning technique.

But do not ask for explanations of your unsuccess. You are better off that rejection slips do not give all the reasons. For, in a market where the Lydia Pinkham pickup and the headache relief in print still meet the chief demand, you would probably get from publishers' readers misleading advice. Some would suggest devices of their favorite recent authors. Others might lay down rules from the style book of a magazine. None can give directions fit to supersede your increasingly exacting taste.

But there is a thing to do. Besides being your own austerest critic, you can seek another to sharpen your self-criticism. Not another critic. If you asked advice from ten intelligent readers you would be told ten different things. Suppose, putting all the suggestions into effect, you still had something left, none of your ten readers would approve. Think what would happen to Shakespeare if all who take picayune exceptions should have their way. Only a few too-often-heard quotations would be left.

Among your acquaintance there must be a man or woman, with tough intelligence and sensitiveness, who, though his main interests are nonliterary, likes you well enough to spend some serious hours with you. Engage him or her to read your piece aloud. Let him read it to himself, first, if he prefers. Several times, if it is verse. Then you can learn by listening as he reads aloud.

Caring more about learning to write than you do about the piece in his hand, you will not blame his reading when passages sound flat. You took it upon yourself to make him see, feel, and imagine, and if his voice goes wrong you have found a place for improving your technique.

In one place your suggestion is too subtle. You can be a little more explicit. In another, you tried to suggest too many things at once. You can spread suggestions thinner. In still another, you can deepen a suggestion not fully taken. By a later stroke, for instance, you can turn the attention back.

Your use of a tangy old idiom produces an unsuitable response. You had forgotten a modern use of the same idiom with a different twist. Or your reader shocks you by a chuckle at a piece of slang. It was apt for what you felt. But since it makes your reader take the sentence in a lower register it will not do. If a similarity that you pointed out now sounds like mere ornament you will delete the metaphor.

Every sentence in which his voice follows your curve of feeling-thought you know is right. Every accent he misplaces, without going back to put it where you meant, shows you a place you may improve. When the reading is done, you have something more useful than praise. Don't let him blur your memory of poor paragraphs and unsuccessful sentences with recommendations of his own. But be grateful that he has helped you hear with a less conspiring ear than yours.

XXXIX

Your punctuation, even, becomes formative

YOU WILL USE more commas when you revise. When someone reads your stuff aloud to you, his mistiming and misphrasing screws you up; you can let the tension go in quarter-twists, sharp prods and strokes, not on your reader's hide but on your manuscript. Like a baseball player, mad at a decision and hitting a two-bagger, you convert your peeve to power. By your reader's maddening inflections you learn how to master his responses; you promptly punctuate in such a way that he will produce a shape of sounds to correspond with what you meant.

Since your sound patterns all match a shape of your experience, punctuation helps define the experience in your readers. Your punctuation co-operates with the natural or habitual suggestiveness of idioms and other live word groups, the way, when you are talking, the expression of your face and body does—and the modulations of your voice.

Since punctuation subtly guides the feeling of relations, the more precise those feelings, the more you punctuate according to them and not according to rules. What indicates precise and delicate relations brings in, always, relativity. And, object who will, punctuation varies with the writer. A student who has memorized forty rules for the use of comma is in for a shock when he reads, for instance, Joseph Conrad. Let him add up all the commas that James Joyce left out. The jar of discovering that rightness in punctuation is imaginative—and measured by response—is one more way of sliding that panel behind the clock. We all live in two realities: one of seeming fixity, with institutions, dogmas, rules of punctuation, and routines, the calendared and clockwise world of all but futile round and round; and one of whirling and flying electrons, dreams, and possibility, behind the clock. The imaginative person has to realize his possibilities *in* the status, the static state of things-as-they-seem, the systematic, organized fiction-fabric of the clockwise world; but he found those possibilities in the still primordial flux, to which dreams, daydreams, and eye-opening events, alike, transport us all. By his daring not to dub the possibilities mere fancies and aberrations, but, instead, to cut away the impracticable parts and to put into (art or) action all the rest, he improves punctuation and, in larger though nearly imperceptible ways, helps create a new civilization in the old culture's arms.

Even the most useful rules, like the one about commas before and after nonrestrictive relative clauses, are not invariable. And you have to feel what will take your reader's mind along with yours.

Recent manuals recommend using commas after an introductory phrase only when the reader would be apt, without the comma, to run the phrase into the principal assertion. As in the sentence, "From characteristic irregularities in behavior patterns have been derived by which certain psychoses can supposedly be recognized." In that sentence a comma after "behavior" is necessary. The expression "behavior patterns" is so jargonically familiar, since behavioristic psychology was invented, that most readers of works on psychology or education would read the two words as a substantive. Then, to make sense, they would be obliged to read the not so rich and rewarding sentence a second time.

"Cut the commas" is an inadequate rule, too. You have to be responsible if you desire response. You cannot have a slide rule and you cannot let the whole matter slide. You have to keep your wits about you and use punctuation, only and always, to beguile your reader into matching the composition that is your thought.

The more idiomatic your speech habits are and the more the turn of the phrase cleaves to the curvature of your personal world—in other words, the more you are an artist—the keener your concern becomes about how you punctuate. The circulation of your meaning is kept smooth and strong by the valves of punctuation.

Even apostrophes are still important when they perform a function. The necessity of pressing down two keys on the typewriter has decreased their use, the same as a backspacing and two separate keys for exclamation points have contributed to the obsolescence of the exclamation. Apostrophes may follow into oblivion the genitive *e* for which they usually stand. But I shall be conservative about them for the same reason that I shall continue to backspace and use two keys in underlining, on those rare occasions when I require italic emphasis or acknowledgment of foreign words. I tried the device, of Bernard Shaw and others, of leaving, instead, two spaces before and after the word or phrase and one space between l e t t e r s. My first reader was "infuriated." She got an impression of showing off and trying to be novel. No small convenience to me can offset such annoyance in a possible reader. I'll save my intransigence for times when more than brief convenience is at stake.

Until I liked one who did it, my own annoyance was

roused by the excessive use of dashes. They are usually intelligible. They are simple. What more do nonpedants want? They want, if they trust words to produce constructive realization, flexibility. And the trouble with dependence on the dash is like the trouble with dependence on a few slang words and phrases: the ways of using are so various that the ways of taking can't be sure.

If differences mean much to you and you have found ways to reconcile where others choose, it will be worth your while to reserve the dash for mild parenthesis, in sentences already using several commas, and for a less rigorous colon. But you had better have an uninhibited colon, too. It is the pair of bars that you can climb over to get a look at the individual trees after you have seen the forest. (It was a variegated stand of trees: oaks, beeches, ash, hornbeam, maple.) Or you can sit on the upper rail and look back at the forest, having come away from individual trees. (The oaks and elms, the balsam, spruce and pine, with here and there a tall white birch: after all his years away, his woodlot still seemed to him a forest.)

The semicolon is the yoke that makes two oxen pull in one direction. Or it is the sawhorse on which a plank is placed so that two kids can teeter. It parts self-sufficient units; it makes one of two.

In punctuation you individualize a social convention, socialize an individual variation. If you are at all like me you will punctuate and unpunctuate as you revise.

XL

Your sentences become increasingly responsive to your ear

WHAT YOU WRITE is dull and awkward when you write because you "have to say something." But when you do a bit of writing that amazes and delights you, its shape incorporating an experience and curving down to earth to affect experience to come, you write because you "have something to say."

Having something to say is like having a baby. First you have it within you, bone of your bone, flesh of your flesh, conceived in passionate opposition. Then with terrific concentration you have it. It becomes self-acting, separate.

The whole process of writing can be like that, in rare and happy moments. But the struggles I have already had on this one page, if nothing else, would force me to acknowledge that often consciousness of how you write is compelled. I have put in, cut out, and stopped and thought. And I have cocked my ear for words and phrases, syllables and stresses that would curve to the sound mold.

The best writing, both prose and poetry, as Shakespeare pre-eminently shows, makes use, with condensation and selection, of playful, impassioned, imaginative talk. If we have the confidence to fit our words and idioms tight around our interior composings when we talk, then we shall write more as life shapes us and we shape our lives. We shall keep the symbiosis of feeling-shape and auditory shape, so that the sound of what we write will evoke the corresponding feelings, the way "Heads up!" gets appropriate action from an American crowd.

But to have a full kit of auditory patterns curved to real emotions we do need to listen. We need to listen, with inside matching on our own part, to those whose phrases fit their inner state. We are lucky if we listen less to lecturers and experts, more to farmers, mechanics, truck drivers, Negro laundresses, and children out of school. The lucky listen to those who have fun when they talk, to born mimics and storytellers, to those whose words, literate or not, play with the people that they talk with, and keep, somehow, in play with the motion of their hearers' minds.

Good sentences do more than state. They may be direct action. Or they may be intricate, composing many sympathies and pressures. All the kinds have the simplicity of a made-up mind. All are natural. They reconcile the mechanical order and the flow of possibility, with a turn of the wrist—like snapping on the electric light.

To get your sentences finally so firm and so alive, you will trust your ear. Often, before they satisfy, you will have to labor and toil, then work some more, destroying every sign of taking pains. But different minds have different difficulties.

Some of us, in the effort to comprehend, catch ourselves with sentences that ignore the paradox that you can't speak the truth when you insist on all the truth. You have to induce your reader to find the context in himself. You show him leaf and bark, make a gesture for the wineglass shape, and let him recognize the tree.

The rationalizing intellect makes difficulty for the imagination. But the life-composing writer has to respect both the reality that never stays put and the fiction of our cut and dried arrangements. Though he has to keep refreshing his concept-ridden speech by exposure to the natural and human differences and changes that make words and logic false, yet he must know the points of the compass, reckon according to the multiplication table, and retain his honest reverence for test tube and telescope. Good sentences ignore nothing human. Their structure suggests the reconciliation of the measurable and the immeasurable. They domesticate in the timed world a little wild potential from the world behind the clock. Continuing composition in the mind behind the sentence gives the sentence power.

You will never be such a craftsman that you can write with perfected skill. But, even at the start, let your sentences resound. Their resonance may be almost as faint as the sound of dew dropping down a grass stalk. It may be like the reassurance of a mother's "Here I am." It may be the hiss and roar and crackle of a destroying flame.

For the crudest honest sentence is a re-sounding of experience. Have you heard a bright child describe an airplane crash? Have you heard a returned soldier describe his once-more-slept-in bed, at home? Sentences resound when experience is comprehendingly relived. But sentences do more. They affect the shape of experience to come. You say, "Ouch, my toe!" Years later on a mountain trail your resounding syllables sound again and I turn back to kick aside a limb with a protruding stub. Your old pain vibrating again in that remembered cry acts at last.

XLI

The technique of poetry comes to have a correlation with the technique of a life worth living

YES, THAT TITLE takes in a lot of territory. But you will not expect an exploitation. That territory will never become a dust bowl—except to such as see, with great intensity, too little of it. And in this chapter we shall do no more than sniff the breeze that blows offshore, and scrutinize a branch or two that birds bring back. Perhaps a gulf stream will carry fragments that we can scoop up for intimations.

Early in the war a friend of mine quoted Grover Cleveland in support of letting culture go from freshman English, for students in the naval reserve. He said that though, theoretically, culture should not be allowed to vanish from the war curriculum, "We face a condition, not a theory." And, with genuine charm and authentic imagination, he developed the argument for letting all that gives meaning to education go for the sake of practical and immediate needs. It was the timeworn and ever-renewed argument that is always implicit in our travesties of constructive effort. It most often gets put into words by the more imaginative.

The argument that "what 'twere good to do" cannot now be attempted because we face a condition is the *cul-de-sac* of civilization. It makes idealists look silly, realists futile. But however much we may dislike the argument, no experienced person can once for all blow it up and burst it.

We never face anything but conditions. It is the mortal condition to be inwardly and outwardly conditioned. And no theory yet has made provision for all the probable and possible conditions. None ever will. Conditions palliate all compromises, all appeasements, all surrenders. We all make conditions our excuse. Except at the times that we wrest conditions to resources. For creation does not cease. And men participate. But the sole alternative to surrender of all meaning, through compromise that continues motion at the price of treadmill motion, is the manipulation of hampering conditions to liberate new possibilities and create new form.

Nearly all of us do some of that, when we care enough for anyone or anything. Few or none are total compromisers. Those who compose most, compromising not at all on main desires and proving possibilities where failure looms, those are our great.

Readers who have lasted to the closing of this little book will, most of them, agree that artists, in all the arts, have created where less energetic, less incorrigibly desirous men have failed or compromised. But what is the use of artists —aside from ornament and diversion, which compromisers furnish, too—unless what artists prove possible for them they equally prove possible for us?

A great poet, a good poet, is a person who, by nature and by desire, adventures where conditions are untoward. He is not stopped, he is not altogether distorted, he is not paralyzed. He suffers, and he is injured. But he comes through, more, not less, whole than any baby ever started. His form embraces conditions and, not conforming to them, bends them, to his continually renewing form. In doing so he may have lost everything except what really matters. And all that was impossible to his nature is still, of course, not there. But he has made a meaning. He has grown into a limited, conditioned, yet paradoxically full man.

"Adventures where conditions are untoward," but also chooses his conditions: whom he marries, where he stays, how he gets his income, what attachments and commitments he incurs, and what he goes without. Not an unconditioned choice, not with the mythical free will of exemption from complex forces determining his motives, but with the freedom of shouldered responsibility. He accepts without self-pity, this actual but best poet, all foreseeable and unforeseeable incidents and consequences of even his least considered, most casual choice. He accepts his own folly.

Such formativeness in the poet's living generates the power and grows the substance of his poems. And in the poems, themselves, he willingly incurs and copes with conditions and restraints that match those—not of his life only—of life. He wants the achievement of charm and delight, and the convincingness and order to be as difficult as it is in any other human enterprise.

What he performs must be performed with ease. But it must never be easy. The resistances overcome and forced into co-operations are his proof. They prove that man can be man and have joy, fun, serenity, in a queer, crazy, all but futile world.

He cannot be grand with sustained grandeur. Milton tried, in private life and in *Paradise Lost,* and came as near as anyone could. But grandeur rises from plateau or plain. Even the ocean is variable and the perceptible eyeful of it is sometimes wild, sometimes frisky, sometimes so subtle in its motion that dull perceivers think it dull. Sublimity must relate to the casual and even the ridiculous, to be convincingly sublime. The ridiculousness affects the sublimity and makes it *affected* (when not allowed for). For there is a joker in every pack.

And so the poet often runs the risk of rime. He has his fun and makes his point by putting on the pacing harness of tradition, yet achieving not only grace but increased naturalness. He says what he says the more precisely as he means it, within the artifice. The artificiality disappears and right rimes—whether exact, deliberately off, or "analyzed," so that assonance of the consonants is paired one way and assonance of the vowels another—right rimes reinforce, corroborate, and validate the feeling-meaning. And the poet can mute the rime, by the way the natural speaking of the line glides over the syllable that ends it. When the matching syllable will intensify, just right, the contrast or the connection of the sense, he lets it ring. Good rime is never functionless. If it does not help the feeling it is bad. Good rime checks and eases the flow of feeling. The poet sets up a faint expectation; we listen for a rime. He puts off the satisfaction. He seems to give it but gives it incompletely; the rime comes but with an accent the sense makes light. Then, when relevant resistance has been incurred and mastered he fills us with fulfillment, "even above the brim."

Or he jingles seeming frivolity in our ears, and, with a mischievous, grim or glorious, irrelevance, he uses the rig-a-jig-jig to snatch us up from the slough of despond, or give us a push on through. He dangles us on a jumping-jack string, another time, and drops us at the knees of God.

Or, as Theodore Spencer did, in his beautiful and wise Phi Beta Kappa Anniversary poem, he passes from un-rimed recitative—which poor reading could reduce to thoughtful prose—to stanzas with such pronounced and regular rimes that, until the whole form has obtained ascendancy over the reader, the simple profundity that they express might be mistaken for mere poetry. He runs that risk. But he succeeds in subduing the strict and formal pattern to his meaning, so that what we get is not verse but an experience. We have moved. With him we have moved.

The poet's ear and his feelings are in accord. And what he cares for most is in the curves and shades of tone. He makes happenings, and the feelings that those happenings produce in him, realizable in the sounds that he combines. His sounds compose to prove that differences of feeling are real as taxes. Every syllable plays a double or a triple role, and, at the line-end, another, in the rime.

Meter, also, is an artificiality and a constraint. Great poems have been written without it. But if poetry is a Jacob's ladder with points sticking through into the dream world, meter is the rungs. Meter acknowledges time, it imposes measure, and implies the confidence of the poet that change and chance and freedom can be known by men who meet payrolls or punch time clocks.

The magic and the fun are not in spite of meter. They are because of the momentary triumphant joining of traditional, man-made order and the flow. For a moment security and possibility unite. Fictions that we treat as hard and fast clasp with fluid reality that we desire and fear.

Meter never makes a good poet lie. It never makes him say what he does not stand and run by. Often it exacts a scouring of resources; he comes upon new clarities because of the exigent time beats.

The breath-pause, or caesura, near the middle of the line, is a similar resource. It is, again, regularity that varies. And the way the feeling places it, now to the left, nearer the beginning of the line, now to the right, nearer to the end, and now in the middle, makes the lines responsive and alive, at the same time that something comfortingly familiar is certain to be reached. Pope makes the otherwise mechanical couplets free and flexible by the right feeling with which, at his best, he makes caesuras fall.

Another technical requirement of poetry, that only they who have the fullest unison between their living and their art can without condescending meet, is readability. For it is absurd to say the poet is too wise to be understood by any but disciples. He is given lots of time. He may write what will be enjoyed after he is no longer around to hear the response. But, soon or late, wisdom works. Otherwise, the poetry may contain much wisdom, but it is not wise enough. The poet is not wise enough to make his poetry reach intelligent people whom he could not teach to read; then he is not wise enough to write the much-considering, much-composing poetry that he tried to write. It is too bad. Possibly if he had not been pampered by other poets, too soon, he might have kept up his struggle and learned, in writing what readers do not know enough to know they want, how to place and light the emotional colors of their common memories and so help them see his picture of the world.

I would rather write Bill Cunningham's column, which is the work of a real man, feeling and, rather crudely and sporadically, thinking for himself and for us all, than write poems liked by twenty, with secret reservations, read enviously and without conviction or delight by fifty and glanced at, skimmed and forgotten by two hundred. Given time, poetry that wins no more and no better reading is not good poetry, no matter how sensitive the poet, no matter how subtle and deft his ear, no matter how fresh his patternings.

Do not lose your humor, no matter how long your forced apprenticeship. Do not blame the times, the public, or influences corrupting taste. These are the best times there are for moving mountains. And poetry that cannot work miracles is not and never was authentic. Your obstacles must become your opportunity.

You still have all the sounds the speaking voice can make, as your material. You still have ways to find what feelings still accompany the sounds. With those two elements, if you can feel enough and still give order to your feelings, you can write, and write for many men. Do not listen to those who sigh and say that poetry is too near the animal and the primitive on the one hand and too elevated and aspiring on the other for our war-torn, economically overturned, and superficially intellectual age. Of course it is. Therein is your opportunity.

These are the times you have to live. These are the times you achieve a meaning or become nearly meaningless. If poetry gives you something, and you want to write, then, without anyone drilling you in technique, your affection and your desire will achieve poems. You will discover, select, contrive, and, first turning experience in these times to significance for more living of your own, will learn — with syllables that catch our cravings and our quakings, our loving and our hating, our failing and our still desiring, with rhythms that match our tensions and relaxings — to show us how you stay alive. Your poetry will have your living form. And, forming with you, readers will gain their minute of composure and just a breath of confidence for the long succession of composings that is staying alive.

A NOTE ON THE AUTHOR

SIDNEY COX *was born in Lewiston, Maine, in 1889. He received his A.B. from Bates College in 1911 and his A.M. from the University of Illinois in 1913. During the First World War he served as a second lieutenant in the infantry and the air service. He taught English for a number of years at Columbia University and the University of Montana, and from 1926 until his death in 1952 was a professor of English at Dartmouth College. His books include* Swinger of Birches: A Portrait of Robert Frost.

A NOTE ON THE TYPE

This book is set in GRANJON, *a type named in compliment to Robert Granjon, type-cutter and printer—in Antwerp, Lyons, Rome, Paris—active from 1523 to 1590. The boldest and most original designer of his time, he was one of the first to practice the trade of type-founder apart from that of printer.*

This type face was designed by George W. Jones, who based his drawings upon a type used by Claude Garamond (1510–61) in his beautiful French books, and more closely resembles Garamond's own than do any of the various modern types that bear his name.

Nonpareil Books

NONPAREIL BOOKS

FICTION:

Frederick Busch:
The Mutual Friend
222 pages; $9.95

Stanley Elkin:
The Franchiser
360 pages; $6.95
Searches and Seizures
320 pages; $6.95

Paula Fox:
Desperate Characters
176 pages; $8.95

William Gass:
*In the Heart of the Heart of the Country
& Other Stories*
240 pages; $7.95
(See also *Literature/Belles Lettres*)

Leslie George Katz:
Fairy Tales for Computers
260 pages; $7.95

William Maxwell:
The Folded Leaf
288 pages; $8.95
Time Will Darken It
320 pages; $9.95
Over by the River
256 pages; $8.95

Howard Frank Mosher:
Disappearances
272 pages; $8.95

Liam O'Flaherty:
Famine
480 pages; $9.95; $18.95 hardcover

Edmund Wilson:
Memoirs of Hecate County
472 pages; $7.95

LITERATURE/BELLES LETTRES:

Brendan Behan:
Borstal Boy
384 pages; $8.95

Sidney Cox:
*Indirections: For Those Who Want to
Write*
160 pages; $5.95

Benedetto Croce:
Aesthetic
544 pages; $9.95

Kennedy Fraser:
The Fashionable Mind
320 pages; $10.95

William Gass:
Fiction and the Figures of Life
304 pages; $7.95
The World Within the Word
352 pages; $7.95

Donald Hall:
String Too Short to Be Saved
176 pages; $7.95

HISTORY:

Warren Chappell:
A Short History of the Printed Word
288 pages; $9.95

Will Cuppy:
*The Decline and Fall of
Practically Everybody*
256 pages; $8.95

Claire Sterling:
*The Masaryk Case: The Murder of
Democracy in Czechoslovakia*
380 pages; $9.95

NATURAL HISTORY:

Clare Leighton:
Where Land Meets Sea
208 pages; $8.95

Donald Culross Peattie:
An Almanac for Moderns
416 pages; 12 wood engravings; $8.9
$17.95 hardcover

Franklin Russell:
Watchers at the Pond
272 pages; Illustrated; $7.95

AMERICANA:

Daniel Carter Beard:
The American Boy's Handy Book
448 pages; 324 figures and 57 line
drawings; $9.95

Armstrong Sperry:
All Sail Set
192 pages; $7.95

All *Nonpareils* are printed on acid-free paper that will not yellow or deteriorate with age. All are bound in signatures, usually sewn, that will not fall out or disintegrate. They are permanent softcover books, designed for use and intended to last for as long as they are read.